FILMMAKERS SERIES

edited by
ANTHONY SLIDE

In Preparation

The Memoirs of
Alice Guy Blaché

translated by
Roberta and Simone Blaché

edited by
Anthony Slide

FILMMAKERS, NO. 12

The Scarecrow Press, Inc.
Metuchen, N.J., & London
1986

Library of Congress Cataloging-in-Publication Data

Guy, Alice, 1873-1968.
    The memoirs of Alice Guy Blaché.

    Translation of: Autobiographie d'une pionnière du
cinéma, 1873-1968.
    Includes index.
    1. Guy, Alice, 1873-1968. 2. Moving-picture
producers and directors--Biography. I. Slide, Anthony.
II. Title.
PN1998.A3G9713 1986   791.43'0233'0924 [B]   86-10099
ISBN 0-8108-1902-3

CONTENTS

To the French she is known as Alice Guy. Americans knew
her as Alice Guy Blaché. Whatever one chooses to call her,
she is not only the cinema's first woman director but also one
of its true pioneers. Her career in the film industry dates
back to the last years of the nineteenth century in France.
She had a glorious beginning as the Gaumont Company's only
director, helping the careers of Ferdinand Zecca, Victorin
Jasset and Louis Feuillade, men whose names were to become
synonymous with the greatness of early French cinema. Yet
somehow along the way, while Zecca or Feuillade were remembered, Alice Guy was forgotten. A pioneer is one who opens
up the way for others to follow, and, for too long, it has
been the followers who received the praise. It is an unfortunate truth that Alice Guy Blaché's career ended on a less
than glorious note here in the United States of America, where
after more than twenty years in an industry which she helped
to create, she could no longer find work.

Between 1897 and 1907, Alice Guy was a leader of the
French film industry. In 1907, she came to the United States,
and, three years later, formed the Solax Company, with headquarters in Fort Lee, New Jersey. In 1913, Alice Guy's hus-
band--Herbert Blaché--formed Blaché Features, half of the
films for which were directed by his wife. (Alice Guy and
Herbert Blaché-Bolton were married in 1907; as soon as the
couple moved to the United States they dropped the Bolton.)
Madame Blaché's last two films were The Great Adventure
(1918) and Tarnished Reputations (1920), both released by
Pathé. The last film which Alice Guy Blaché was invited to
direct was one of the "Tarzan" features; she declined the offer.

It is perhaps not unfair to suggest that Herbert Blaché
was in part responsible for the demise of his wife's directorial

v

career. He promoted himself over and above his wife wherever possible, even having her work as his assistant. The writing was on the wall as early as 1913 when Blaché forced the closure of the Solax Company, so closely associated with Alice Guy Blaché, and in its place formed his own organization, Blaché Features.

Another, and equally important, factor in Alice Guy Blaché's relative obscurity has been the nonexistence of any of her American features. Although a dozen or so of the Solax short subjects have survived--notably in the collection of the Library of Congress--none of the features is known to be extant. Without them it is difficult to reinforce the argument for recognition of Alice Guy Blaché as a major director in the American film industry of the teens. One longs to view one of the features she made with Madame Olga Petrova, highly regarded as a great dramatic actress in her day and a staunch feminist who insisted on strong female roles for her films.

I first became aware of the existence of Alice Guy Blaché's memoirs on April 10, 1973, when I visited her daughter, Simone, at her then-home in Mahwah, New Jersey. Simone entrusted the autobiography to me, and, happily, I was able to arrange for its publication in French by Denoël/Gonthier in 1976. I had long hoped that an English-language edition might be possible, and, to my great delight, Simone and her sister-in-law, Roberta, agreed to translate Alice Guy Blaché's memoirs for this Scarecrow Press publication.

In editing Alice Guy Blaché's memoirs, I have removed an introductory chapter in which the author discussed the various inventions which led up to the creation of the French film industry. I have also deleted some material from the end of the manuscript, which I felt to be erroneous and which did not deal directly with Alice Guy Blaché's career. All the words are Alice Guy Blaché's. I have not added anything to the text except for material placed within brackets.

After some consideration, Simone Blaché and I decided that this should be called the "Memoirs of Alice Guy Blaché" rather than "Alice Guy." It was our feeling that she was known as Alice Guy Blaché in America, and as this book is being published here it was appropriate to use the "Blaché." For the French edition, the name Alice Guy was used.

Finally, I would like to express my thanks to Nicole-Lise Bernheim and Claire Clouzot, who edited the French edition of this book and who were instrumental in its publication in Paris. Special thanks are also due to Francis Lacassin, who so generously gave permission for the publication here of his listing of Alice Guy's French films. And last, my personal thanks to Simone Blaché, who kept the faith for so many years and worked so hard, and yet so quietly, to keep her mother's memory alive.

Anthony Slide

CHAPTER ONE

In an era in which "retrospectives" are fashionable, perhaps
the souvenirs of the eldest of women film directors may find
some favor with the public. I have no pretense to making a
work of literature, but simply to amuse, to interest the reader
by anecdotes and personal memories concerning their great
friend the cinema, at whose birth I assisted.

I have often been asked why I chose so unfeminine a
career. Yet, I have not chosen this career. No doubt my
destiny was traced before my birth and I have merely followed
a Will whose name I do not know. Strange fate! which I
shall try to recount for you.

I was born on the first of July, 1873, in the Parisian
suburb of Saint-Mande, two steps from the Bois de Vincennes.

In order that one of her children should be French (my
numerous brothers and sisters had all been born in Chile),
my mother had valiantly endured a sea voyage of seven weeks.
Thus I also accomplished my first voyage between Valparaiso
and Paris. It was not to be my last.

At that time such a crossing was an adventure. Seven
weeks in a comfortless boat! What motive could have made
my parents exile themselves in that way?

In 1847 or 1848 an uncle and an aunt of my mother had
emigrated to South America, in order to rebuild a fortune
much shaken by the Revolution. Having succeeded beyond
their hopes, they wished to see again their family and their
country.

There they made the acquaintance of my mother, their
niece, who was then a student in the Convent of the Visitation. Charmed by her beauty, and themselves rich and child-
less, they begged my grandparents to confide her to their

care. They hoped to marry her to a friend and compatriot,
Emile Guy, of a good Franc-Comtois family (my paternal grandmother was the aunt of Etienne Lamy) founder of the first
bookshops in Valparaiso and Santiago. I have been told that
an Emile Guy bookstore still exists in Santiago.

Three months later the marriage was celebrated in Paris
at the Church of the Madeleine.

I do not know if love had a part in the arrangement.
At that period, a family decided the future of its daughters.
The austere Convent of the Visitation primarily insisted on
the accomplishment of the Christian duties. A proper woman
must obey her husband, keep her house well, and care for
her children. Culture was considered secondary, if not a
liability.

Some days later my grand-uncle and his wife turned back
toward Chile, accompanied by the newlyweds. The voyage
must have been a harsh trial for my poor mama: to leave her
country and her beloved parents for a distant country whose
language she could not speak, and for companions a husband
and relations who had been unknown a few weeks earlier, and
with all that she was terribly seasick. But she kept brave
and strong.

When she arrived in Valparaiso the whole French colony
wished to be presented to her and my grand-uncle gave her
as a wedding gift the keys of a fine house as luxuriously
furnished as the resources of the country permitted.

She promised to do her utmost to repay so much kindly
interest, learned Spanish quickly, and offered her help to
my father in his affairs. He entrusted her with some books
received from France, asking that she should review them for
him, and she accomplished this task very well. Her gracious
hospitality, her devotion to the unfortunate, made her the
rage of the French colony.

All the Europeans feared the still-untamed Chilean Indians
but the Indians adored my mother for her goodness and the
mere tales of her encounters with them are of interest.

She was twenty-six years old when she decided that her
fifth child should be truly French, of French birth.

As soon as they were old enough to travel my brother
and sisters were sent to France, to the care of the Jesuits,
to receive the only education judged proper at that time.

My father who had accompanied them returned to Chile
shortly after my birth. My mother rejoined him some months
later and I was confided to the care of my maternal grandmother. This abandonment caused me no harm: my grandmother loved and spoiled me. She lived in Carouge, a Geneva
suburb dear to artists, in a little apartment whose terrace
gave on one of those scented, disorderly gardens, bordered
by the Rhone. It was there that my older brother and my
three sisters took refuge during school vacations or in case
of illness.

Grandmother was not wealthy, however in her tiny lodging in spite of our differences in age, we were each happy.
Gathered around her table where the cherry soup, fragrant
with hot wine and cinnamon, or the white cheese she made
herself offered its goodness in a bowl of cream, she recounted
the legends of her native Bérnais region and sang for us in
her admirable voice, astonishingly young, her favorite song:
"Beau ciel de Pau quand donc te reverrai-je." Thus it was
a shock when three years later my mother, whom I had forgotten, came to see us and decided to take me to Valparaiso.
In the railroad station my poor grandmother wept. I cried,
too, and threw a tantrum, but the departure signal hastened
our separation. Drunk with tears, I slept at last.

Our places were reserved on an English cargo vessel;
I don't know if we left from Havre or from Bordeaux but the
novelty of the surroundings, the activity of the travelers,
porters, sailors, the sight of the great sailing-ship on which
we were going to voyage had already pushed into the past
the face of my grandmother.

In those days, the ship had to carry all the necessities
of life for nearly two months. The deck became a veritable
farmyard. A crane transferred sacks and barrels into the
hold. All the voyagers were supplied with deck-chairs, and
plaid blankets, and my mother, already miserable, had at
once handed me over to the one chambermaid.

The only child on board, I quickly became the pet of
the passengers and crew. My mother remained stretched on

her deck-chair, willingly leaving me to the care of the other
passengers, with whom, despite the difference of language,
I had a perfect understanding. Perhaps I already used
pantomime!

Of this voyage I have kept few memories. The long gold
ribbon that the moon unrolled to the horizon. The phosphores-
cent sea, the flying fish, my own baptism on crossing the
Equator.

At Saint-Vincent in the Bahamas where the harbor swarmed
with sharks the passengers threw coins in the sea for the
native children to dive and capture. I was too young to
understand the cruelty of this sport. Happily, the sharks
were slow to return and the little blacks, lively and adroit,
escaped without damage.

In Rio de Janeiro, in Buenos Aires, we stopped several
days to renew our provisions and to let the passengers rest.
The Panama Canal did not yet exist, the passage across the
Andes was unthinkable for a woman and child. We sailed
coast-wise along Patagonia, and I remember that a native of
Tierra del Fuego, nearly nude but wearing a superb opera
hat, climbed onto the bridge.

At last we entered the Strait of Magellan and for me the
fairy-tale began. The ship advanced slowly, prudently, between two walls of ice. From every crevice the sun struck
iridescent sparks and my childish imagination peopled every
cavern, every frozen cascade, with fairies and strange beasts.
I felt certain I had seen polar bears come by moonlight to
watch our passage. My mother assured me there was no bear,
no fairy, there. Even today, I am not so sure; I have seen
them so often in dreams...

Finally we came out into the Pacific and turned north-
ward, following the coast of Chile to Valparaiso where my
father awaited us.

The arrival was full of interest for me. The port of
Valparaiso not permitting large ships to enter; numerous little
Indian boats paddled to meet us. Most carried the flowers
and fruits of the country: mangos, cherimoyas, offered to
the voyagers by means of little baskets fixed to the end of
poles. Cranes were installed to help passengers, animals and
baggage to be lifted and deposited on the wharf.

I had installed myself astride the rail of the ship the better to follow the spectacle. The cabin-boy, sent to find me, pulled me from this perilous position and conducted me to my mother whom I found, to my profound astonishment, in the arms of a tall gentleman who kissed her repeatedly and then examined her with care: "The voyage has tired you, my poor Marie," he said, "you don't look well."

"Nothing surprising in that, Mister Guy," said the captain, approaching us. "Missia Mariquita is brave but seven weeks of sea-sickness take their toll. I really thought we ought to have left her in Rio. By contrast," said he, hugging me, "here is a little girl who doesn't fear the ship's rolling. Really a sea dog!"

My father...for the gentleman with the Gallic moustache was my father...seemed to notice me for the first time. He drew me near him and looked long at me.

"She resembles you, Marie" he said at last, embracing me.

"That's true, Missia Mariquita," said the captain. "Let's hope she'll grow up as good and beautiful as you."

"You are not going to Europe this year, Don Emilio?"

"No. I have just opened another bookstore in Santiago and that needs all my attention."

After a few words of thanks and farewell we were, in our turn, installed in the landing bark. On the quay servants waited for us. They had copper-colored skin, black hair, straight and shining, and fine eyes a bit slanted, shining with joy, and from their mouths with the dazzling teeth came words: "Buenos días, Missia Mariquita: ¿Como esta? Que bonita la niñita!"

They settled us in a light cabriolet drawn by two little horses. My father seized the reins and we started off at full trot through the shady streets, passing poncho-clad Indians and lovely Chilean women in mantillas.

Soon the carriage halted before a vast "hacienda." My father tossed the reins to a servant who had rushed up, and

he carried (rather more than aided) my mother to the large
porch protected from the sun by a thatch of woven reeds.
Refreshments had been set out near a chaise longue on which
my mother stretched out with delight. Left to myself, turned
loose, I resolved to explore this new world and set off bravely
down a corridor at the end of which I could hear voices and
laughter. It opened on a veranda giving on a great court
where servants were unloading the baggage. They noticed
me and approached. One of the Indian women wanted to pick
me up. Terrified, I fled screaming and bumped into my mother
who had hurried after me, thinking there had been an acci-
dent. She understood what had happened and, taking me in
her arms, signalled the crestfallen Indian to come close.

"Don't be afraid, little one," she told me. "Conchita
is sweet and kind; she's the one who will take care of you.
Give her your hand."

I obeyed. Conchita gently took my hand and kissed it.
Emboldened, I gazed at her and soon held out my arms. From
that hour we were inseparable.

It was she who, that evening, put me to bed in the big
willow basket which served me as a cradle, after having heard
my prayers. She sang, to put me to sleep, an Indian lullaby.

I grew quickly accustomed to my new life. I saw very
little of my parents. My father was preoccupied by his affairs, my mother busy with her social and charitable duties.
I passed most of my time in the great laundry room where
Conchita met her friends after she had dressed me and taken
me for my walk. In Chile, in those days at least, every house
had its private laundry. In a country where the heat is intense and it rarely rains one must change one's linen daily,
and the clothes of women are light in color. Our servants
were young and gay, they sang from morning to night. A
big demi-john of the local wine served to refresh them. Profiting one day by a moment of inattention on the part of Conchita, I tasted that and found it so good that soon I swayed
on my little legs. Conchita perceived my condition without
understanding it. Very troubled, she led me to my mother.
I breathed, it seems, a perfume so wine-laden that my mother
knew at once what was wrong with me. She scolded us
sharply, Conchita for her failure to watch me, and I for my
debauchery. But my usual shyness was diluted by the drink;

I ran about on my cottony legs, lifting my arms to heaven
and crying "What a fuss for a little glass of wine!" I was
put to bed and I slept immediately, but when I returned to
the laundry someone had put the bottle out of reach.

I liked Sunday very much. At Mass there were always
big baskets full of blessed brioches. I liked to see the
beautiful Chilean women kneeling on their little mats laid directly on the ground, their arms sometimes crossed, lost in
profound adoration. Afternoons, I climbed with Conchita
among the cliffs overhanging the bay. There the old Indian
women with the aid of big round stones ground corn in the
hollows of rock. They made succulent impanades, a sort of
turnover stuffed with meat, pimento, and dried grapes. They
sold loaves of maple sugar, and enormous oranges. Their
clothes were many-colored and their tongues were active. We
would go home at nightfall.

I was on good terms with the night-watchman, of whom
I had been afraid that first night when I heard his voice
crying the hours and who had come to our aid one day when
an earthquake (something, alas, frequent in Chile) completely
rearranged the furniture.

I had made the acquaintance of Quatrocentimos, the
heroic fire-house dog, the firemen's mascot, who seized the
broken hoses in his jaws and held them firmly until the men
had finished their work. This extraordinary animal went beg-
ging from door to door. He accepted only pennies. When he
had four of these he would go to the butcher or baker and
could very well indicate the morsel he wanted. For this he
was named Quatrocentimos (Four Cents).

Sometimes he paid us a visit. If I were in the patio he
lay down and I might play at will between his paws until his
duties called him elsewhere. He loved the patio, as I did.
Strange flowers grew there, whose names I did not know,
but whose penetrating perfumes I have since recognized sometimes, in the course of my travels, and each time they have
evoked for me the memory of Chile.

After two years of this happy life full of gaiety, of
sunshine, I had become a black little person, speaking only
Spanish. What happened at that moment? What drama crossed
our life? I still don't know.

One morning, Conchita came weeping to wake me and
I was dressed more warmly than usual. Baggage was piled
up on the veranda. My mother pressed me in her arms, kiss-
ing me over and over. My father was already seated in the
same cabriolet that had carried us two years earlier, and it
was with him alone that I sadly made the return voyage.

Again we took the route by the Strait of Magellan, in
reverse. My wonderment did not have the same freshness, I
was missing mama and Conchita. My father, very grave,
spoke little. However, once again the life aboard made me,
little by little, forget my grief. The ship transported animals
for a zoological garden: two little lion cubs, and a splendid
condor whom I tried to feed strawberries and who nearly removed my hand.

At last we arrived in Bordeaux. I shall never forget
the night we passed in the hotel there. My father had ordered
a drink. He stared unseeingly at the golden liquid and great
tears rolled into his moustache. Seated on a little stool near
his armchair, I watched, with a heavy heart, his hand droop-
ing near me against which I longed, but did not dare, to lay
my cheek.

Some days later I was enrolled as a student at the Con-
vent of the Sacred Heart, at Viry, on the Swiss border. I
was six years old. After those two years of sun and gaiety,
I seemed to have entered the world of the night-birds. The
Count of Viry had loaned his castle to the Sisters exiled from
France. The black-clad nun who received me made me mount
and descend stairways, traverse long, vaulted, dark corridors.
The silence was absolute, the cold penetrating.

In the big, parsimoniously lighted dormitory we entered,
little girls dressed in long nightgowns knelt before their beds,
responding to the rosary monotonously ticked off by a gover-
ness. A young girl wearing the dark blue uniform...which
would also be mine...with the light blue ribbon and silver
medal of the Children of Mary, took my hand and led me to
a little empty bed, undressed me and put me to bed, where,
sobbing, I finally slept.

At six o'clock Mass I found my three sisters and felt
less forsaken. Breakfast took place in the refectory where
long tables were laid for us. The nuns passed behind us,
distributing bread and cafe au lait. We ate in silence, while
an older girl read us a pious lecture.

I learned French again and submitted to the hard transformation of a free, gay baby into a timid, well-behaved little
girl. The methods used were without softness. For the
smallest offense there were long periods of kneeling, arms
crossed, in an icy corridor. For graver sins, a cell and dry
bread and water. But the Sisters were not cruel. The Order
was a strict one for them, also. The superior, a very great
lady, wished to make us into strong, accomplished women,
capable of conducting themselves correctly in any rank of
society. To that end she employed the means of that era.

My only truly happy days were those when I was ill.
I often suffered tonsillitis and the nuns, doubtless fearing
the contagion, asked my grandmother to come fetch me. That
was a week of grace in which I tasted tenderness again.

We enjoyed, however, my sisters and I, a certain favor:
we four were the protegées of Monseigneur Merlinod, then
bishop of Geneva, and family friends.

I passed six years in that somber house. Every Thursday we took a walk in the neighboring countryside, which was
quite pretty. We strolled two by two under the eye of a lay-
sister. The favorite amusement of some of my companions
froze me with horror, for it was the hunt for frogs which
they skinned and threw back, still alive, into the pond, a
game which our guardian watched with indifference.

The Fourteenth of July was a sad day. At every fire-
work which rang out in the village, we had to drop to our
knees and pray for the soul of Louis XVI.

When the big girls left on vacation they were warned
that if they should kiss a boy they would grow a superb
moustache. I have since then found a branch of my Convent
in the United States. Things have changed, indeed. Now,
the nuns themselves prepare the students for their dates,
and teach them dancing.

A series of catastrophes put an end to our imprisonment.
In Chile violent earthquakes, fire and theft ruined my parents.
My father returned alone to France. He gathered up with
him my brother and two eldest sisters and we, my last sister
and I, were placed in a less expensive convent at Ferney, in
the ancient château of Voltaire, properly exorcised. Who

knows if his shade did not wander sometimes in the garden or
the rooms, listening with irony to our lessons....

The death of my elder brother, carried off at seventeen
by a rheumatic heart, brought my mother back to France and
reunited us all in Paris, in living conditions very different
from those we had known. My eldest sister entered l'Ecole
normale, the two others were hastily married. I finished my
studies in a little class on the rue Cardinet, while my father
died at fifty-one, more broken by sorrow than by illness.

I remained alone with my mother, who had never until
then had to occupy herself with the realities of life.

However, he had kept several friends. Thanks to them,
my mother was named director of the Mutualite maternelle, a
society created by the textile unions to aid needy women
workers entering on maternity, social security being nonex-
istent in those days.

Her experience gained in the Chilean hospitals where
she had charitably contributed her time served as an excellent
preparation for the task which now fell to her. My mother devoted herself whole heartedly.

Thinking that contact with true misery could only be
healthful for me, my mother took me with her to aid in her
work. My debut was difficult. I was to perfection the little
white goose of the period. A bit of a snob, I felt the sub-
urban people to be a different class of being. A few visits
sufficed to waken my sympathy, my pity, often my admiration.

When I carried to Professor Dehenne in his ophthalmology
clinic in the rue Monsieur-le-Prince newborn babies with running eye infections that a wait of a few hours might have
rendered blind, it was with not a little pride that I heard
the master say "Ah! Here is Miss Alice with her children...."

After having cared for the babies he took my hand and
washed my eyes with argyrol: "Take care, my dear. That
nastiness is terribly contagious. It must not spoil these
pretty eyes."

Some months later, following a disagreement with the
administration, my mother resigned her post and we found

ourselves once again in a difficult situation. But we had a
new friend: the secretary-general of the Syndicate, nephew
of the foundress of the convent where we had been educated.
"P.B." must have been seventy years old then. I was seventeen, but I was perfectly charmed by him.

Every Thursday evening was a party for me. We passed those evening in P.B.'s home with his two daughters. I
sat close to him, my hand in his, while his two daughters
served tea or played music and my mother knitted or embroidered.

It was P.B. who advised my mother to have me take
typing and stenography lessons, a science quite new in those
days. The course director was an excellent legal stenographer
for the Chamber of Deputies, where he sometimes led me, as
well as at the Sorbonne. Having remarked on my rather
rapid progress, he decided to give me private lessons. Very
soon he judged me ready to take a secretarial post in a little
factory in the Marais neighborhood of Paris, "to polish you"
he said. "When I find something better I'll let you know."

This first secretarial job, rue of the Quatre-Fils, in a
varnish factory, was certainly a grinding and polishing one.
My employers occupied an office separate from the great room
where I found the foreman, the accountants, and myself.
After having opened the mail, the foreman would leave to
distribute the day's orders to the various workshops.

I stayed alone among a dozen men. One of them was
an African Legionnaire and I assure you he was neither handsome nor blond...and that the sun did not kiss the brow of
mon Legionnaire! He had a great mouth full of black teeth,
from which came as from a gutter, all sorts of army-camp
pleasantries, evidently addressed to me. I understood enough
so that one day, exasperated, I ran to his desk where, beating my fist with all my force I shouted at him "You can swallow
that stuff, hold your tongue and let me work in peace or I'll
tell someone who can make you do so." He jumped up like a
jack-in-the-box. "Why, shit, listen to her attack me! We'll
have to break the kid in," he said.

The foreman's arrival interrupted the dialogue. I regained my place, still trembling and near tears. Contrary to
my expectations, I didn't see him when we left work but the

next day I was called into the boss's office and he said
severely "Mademoiselle, you are here as a secretary. It is
not your place to correct the staff as it seems you did, yesterday. Try not to let it happen again."

"Pardon, Sir, I did not correct the staff on the subject
of work."

"Really? On what subject, then?"

Unwillingly, I described the scene.

"I understand better, but why didn't you speak to your
foreman or to me?" he asked. He rang for the foreman.
"Call in so-and-so." A few minutes later "my Legionnaire"
appeared, much less jaunty. "Mademoiselle has just given me
a version of yesterday's scene, different from yours," the
boss told him. "If you want to keep you job, see that she
needn't complain again. You may go." Without answering,
but with a hard look at me, he turned on his heel. I offered
my thanks and went back to my own place.

All the employees were not so vulgar. One of the young
accountants willingly helped me when the filing was too heavy.
He profited by the first favorable moment to whisper: "Let
me accompany you, this evening. He has threatened to make
you pay dearly for what happened. He is bad, really."

"Thank you. You are kind, but at seven o'clock the
streets are not empty. He won't eat me."

We were in winter, one of the coldest that I've known.
On leaving the office I found the night was black and when
I heard a heavy step behind me it was not only the freezing
air that made me shiver. But for nothing in the world would
I hasten my walk. He caught up with me quickly and in his
most common voice opened a dialogue:

"Will it bother you if I walk with you?"

"The sidewalk is for everyone."

"Well, now we can gab!"

"You're the one who's gabbing, as you say. You've

spit in the air and it's fallen back on your nose. Too bad
for you."

"No kidding...you shouldn't have complained...right?"

"No indeed. I thought I could defend myself alone
against your insults. What you did was ugly, you know."

I was no longer afraid and my anger rose again. I
told him everything I felt about the incident. He listened
with a crestfallen air, shaking his shoulders now and then
like a wet dog.

Finally he stopped me. "Alright, dear. You're right.
Since you seem like a good girl we can be friends if you
will...them if somebody bothers you he'll have to deal with me."

He offered me his big paw...I gave him mine. Certainly
to the great surprise of my friend the accountant who was
following us at a distance. He kept his word, and I finished
my time at the factory in peace.

CHAPTER TWO

In March 1895, if my memory is exact,* a note from my stenography professor informed me that the Comptoir général de Photographie was seeking a secretary. A warm letter of recommendation accompanied the note.

Was this the chance we had waited for so long?

Thus, with beating heart and high hopes I entered the building at 57 rue Saint-Roch, at the corner of the avenue of the Opera, hiding as best I could the torn pocket of my winter coat.

First disappointment: the employee to whom I spoke informed me that the director, M. Richard, was out. Then, seeing my discomfiture: "You might perhaps see his representative, M. Gaumont.** I'll go see if he can receive you."

Some moments later he led me into a large windowed room. Behind a big desk a man, still young, of energetic aspect, was writing. I had no idea that I had known him a long time.

In fact, while I followed the course in typing and stenography, we had rented a little apartment on the rue de Tournon. In a building at a little distance I often noticed a window which remained lighted a good part of the night. It was, I believe, that of a young student finishing his engineering studies while working for the Carpentier company. I must have met him every day, perhaps going toward the Luxembourg park, perhaps going down the Boulevard Saint-Michel on my way to class.

---

* It was probably 1894.
** Léon Gaumont (1863-1946) acquired the Comptoir in 1895, and in 1906 it became the Société des établissements Gaumont. The company remains active through the present as a producer and distributor.

The apartment where we live was above that of the celebrated medium Mademoiselle Lenormand. If I had consulted
her at that moment, she would probably have predicted that
I would meet, daily, a young man ten years my senior who
would occupy an important place in my life.

I believe it was at that epoch, or perhaps a few months
later, that Léon Gaumont met Mademoiselle X [Camille Maillard],
daughter of a Belleville landowner who enjoyed a certain
wealth, that he married her and that she brought him a dowry
of large land-holdings on which were built, some years later,
the studios in which the cinema was born.

"What do you wish, Mademoiselle?" he asked, raising
his eyes.

Timidly, I offered him my letter of introduction. He
read it, examined me in silence and finally said:

"The recommendation is excellent, but this post is important. I fear, Mademoiselle, that you may be too young."

All my hopes crumbled.

"But Sir," I pleaded "I'll get over that."

He looked at me again, amused.

"Alas, that's true," he said "you shall get over it.
Well, let's try."

He gave me a note-tablet, and a pencil, and indicated
a chair facing him and he rapidly dictated two or three pages.
In spite of my trembling fingers, I managed without difficulty.

"That's good," he said, "come back this afternoon. If
M. Richard agrees, you may begin tomorrow. The beginning
salary is a hundred and fifty francs. Will that suit you?"

That would suit me very well, as my preceding salary
had been a hundred and twenty-five francs per month...gold
francs, it's true.

"When can you start?"

"This afternoon, Sir, if you wish."

"Good, then. I'll introduce you to M. Richard who must decide."

I had wings, flying home to our little apartment. I rushed to my mother to give her the happy news. How Happy! I did not know the future this beginning held in reserve for me. If I had guessed I might have recoiled from the difficulties of the task.

M. Richard made no difficulty in approving the decision of his representative and I was able soon to take account of the weight and complexity of my work.

In front of one of the windows giving on the avenue of the Opera, a little table was placed for me, with a typewriter. I was surrounded by a screen. An electric bell linked me to the office of the directors and, from eight in the morning until eight at night, six days per week, I had to answer the imperious bell-summons from the directorial desk.

In those days photography reigned. All the aristocrats, all the scientific world, all the artists (writers, painters, sculptors), the diplomatic world and even the demi-monde made photographs. It was the Belle Epoque. Exhibits of amateur work were popular, the most remarkable being printed in the big journals and magazines. Some were truly works of art.

I knew almost nothing of this art. I had to familiarize myself with the sizes of plates, the variety of papers, the chemical products, the different camera names, their qualities, focus-lengths, shutters, etc. Happily, I learned quickly. Soon my employers found that I lost too much time in coming and going and installed me in their own office, which permitted me to know everything that happened in the company and to become acquainted with our principal clients.

There I met such savants as: Eleuthère Elie-Nicolas Mascart, the physicist (in atmospheric electricity and terrestrial magnetism) who, to the great astonishment of Caumont, waited over half an hour in his office simply chatting with me. The doctor Pierre-Paul Emile Roux, disciple and successor of Pasteur, inventor of diphtheria vaccine. Thierry

de Martel, son of Gyp. This famous surgeon, who treated
me and my daughter and showed us great kindness, gave us
the sorrow of learning of his suicide when the Germans
entered Paris. Louis-Paul Cailletet, a physicist who liquefied
gas, air, and oxygen. Arsène d'Arsonval, who used high-
frequency electric currents in medicine, thus creating the
Arsonval currents. Joseph Vallot, astronomer and geographer
who installed his observatory on the summit of Mont Blanc.
He invited me to go up there and offered me guides. Unfortunately, my marriage hindered me from accepting the invitation. The doctor Jean Charcot, celebrated explorer who
perished on the Pourquoi Pas? Salomon-Auguste Andrée, who
left for the North Pole in 1897 in a balloon, and who, until
lately was believed lost without trace.

I have recently read in a book by W. Cross and Th.
Hellbrom, from a condensation published in Lectures pour
tous, that the remains of Andreé and his companions have
been recovered and that they died of trichinosis from having
eaten infected bear meat without cooking it sufficiently. Gas-
ton Bonnier, apiculturist and botanist who raised bees in the
Luxembourg gardens. I have heard him, long before the ap-
pearance of Maeterlinck's book, speak of the intelligence and
industry of bees. The doctor Alexandre Yersin, microbiolo-
gist (whom I, myself, equipped with a film camera on his
departure for Hong-Kong where he discovered the plague
bacillus) and he was as simple and amiable as a college boy.
Gustave Eiffel, engineer who built many bridges and the
Eiffel Tower, and who began the construction of the Panama
Canal. I have kept a pleasant souvenir of him, because of
the encouragement with which he always showered me. C.-A.
François-Franck, director of the Institute, whom I often helped
to photograph ataxic persons, the respiration of animals with
hearts laid open, and frogs which I marked with white flags
before registering their palpitations. François-Franck was
always kind to me, and it was he who got me my first decora-
tion: Chevalier of the Academy. Louis and Auguste Lumière,
who were world renowned. They made me a present of a
portrait of my mother, a color portrait after the Lippmann
process, and I keep it piously. Alberto Santos-Dumont,
Brazilian aviator whose first flight we filmed...a hundred
metres, I believe...at the moment when the Wright brothers
also made their first flight, which they might not have been
able to do without the aid of the Dion-Bouton motor which the
inventor had put at their disposal.

There were writers such as Emile Zola, whom I knew
while he was defending Dreyfus, some time before his death.
He and his wife made an odd couple. Certain things were
published about Zola's life at the time which I can neither af-
firm nor deny. And Octave Mirbeau who worked on <u>le Temps</u>
newspaper. He had created a scandal by publishing the <u>Diary</u>
<u>of a Chambermaid</u>, which would doubtless appear harmless
enough today. It was he who drew Maeterlinck to light, by
writing of him in an article full of high praise for one of the
poems he had sent to his friend Paul Hervieux. Les Cases
was the son of the historian who wrote of Napoleon on the
island of Elba; he often interested us by the memories his
father had left him. The Princess Bibesco, of the Bibesco
family, hospodar of Wallachia; a rather masculine woman, very
dark, with magnificent eyes and a lightly shaded lip. I never
read any of her books.

There were also statesmen: Waldeck-Rousseau, prime
minister, whom I nicknamed "The Owl." He was so amiable,
and his wife was as ill-spoken as a washerwoman. Entering
one of the reception rooms of the Comptoir général de Photographie she cried "But it stinks here!"

René Viviani, son-in-law of Eiffel. He came to America
while I was there. I had known all the Eiffel family, having
received them often in the studio and having organized little
receptions for them. In the course of one of their visits to
the Comptoir, Viviani asked me "Well, Mademoiselle Alice, when
are you going to marry?" I said "I suppose that I love my
work too much. If I decide someday to marry it will only be
to have children." Viviani looked at me with a malicious
smile and answered "One could help you." When René Viviani
came to the United States I was one of the Franco-Belge Circle. All the ladies [of that circle] were eager to be presented
to him, pushing me as far to the rear as they could, However, I would only have had to send him my card, asking him
to do me the honor of visiting my studio, to have that visit.
I abstained. Was I wrong...was I right?

I also want to mention Louis Renault whom I knew as a
simple mechanic, one of whose brothers was killed in the 1903
Paris-Madrid race, I think. Actually his name is known around
the world. [There was] the celebrated Jambon who decorated
the great theatres of Paris (the Opera, the Théâtre Français)
and who decorated the Paris street in the 1900 Exposition, and

with whom I felt a sincere friendship. I shall speak of him
again in the course of these memoirs. Gaillard, director of
the Opera of whom I shall also speak later, and who was
seventy-two years old when I met him for the first time.
Charles-Edouard Guillaume, director of the International
Bureau of Weights and Measures. The two Falize brothers,
two magnificent boys with completely white hair, who after
every homeric bicycle race insisted on having me note their
muscular development. I was happy to see again their splendid shop on the rue de la Paix, when I returned from the
United States.

Also among the clients of the Comptoir were the Duchess
d'Uzes, whose hunt we were to film, and whom I had met already while helping my mother at the Mutualite maternelle.
The Empress Eugenie-Marie of Montijo. I possess among my
souvenirs an umbrella case which she presented to my mother
at some Court gala. After the death of her son killed in an
ambush among the Zulus, she made a visit to the Comptoir
général de Photographie, but was so sad, so diminished, that
I dared not recall to her the memories I had of her. Queen
Ranavalo, the dethroned queen of Madagascar, very dignified,
very sad.

The Marquis and Marquise of Baroncelli-Javon I shall
speak of later. I knew them at Saintes-Maries-de-la-Mer and
surprised them greatly when I told them that in Chile my
parents were linked in friendship with a Baroncelli who was
the French consul. The Marquis raised his arms to Heaven:
"My uncle! She knew my uncle!" "Not I," I answered "but
my parents. In Chile the French grouped together, and
Adelina Patti was among them with others whose names escape
me." The Marquis was very interested in cowboys and I sent
him some post-cards from the United States, hoping to please
him. I also knew d'Alsace, president of the Israelite charity,
noted for his great goodness.

Claude Bromhead, director and then owner of the Gaumont London branch, to my knowledge, took the first pursuit
film with les Braconniers. Monsieur and Madame Dieulafoy,
archeologists and scholars who propagated the taste for Spanish
literature. She was the first woman I had seen wearing
culottes. Frédéric Dillaye, technical adviser for Gaumont
photographic work, employed in a ministry. He had written
numerous books on photography and was my benevolent

professor, especially when I began making films. His family
life was overturned by the terrible fire in the Charity Bazaar
[on May 4, 1897]. The Dillaye family lived in a pretty villa
on the outskirts of Paris. Madame Dillaye was a little late
that day in taking the train which would carry her to the
Charity Bazaar where she kept a stand. The stationmaster,
who knew her, ran with her to open the coach for her and
help her mount into it.

.   Frederic Dillaye was in the Gaumont office. We were
chatting peacefully when an employee, very pale and shaken,
came to warn Gaumont of the disaster begun by the cinema
at the Charity Bazaar. Dillaye heard part of the conversation. He, Gaumont and I, myself, we took a carriage and
hurried to the place of the terrible fire.

People ran wildly on all sides. At last the firemen succeeded in conquering the flames and Dillaye found himself,
by chance, beside one of his daughters who had just ran
madly forth from the blaze. She told him she had been hold-
ing her mother's hand at the moment of escape. A movement
of the crowd had separated them and she asked what had happened to her mother.

Useless to say what horror we suffered, up until the
moment when, very late at night, people were admitted to try
and recognize the remains of the victims. I was not author-
ized to accompany Gaumont and Dillaye, nor would I have had
the courage to do so. It was only after long searching, and
only by her earrings, that Frederic Dillaye recognized the
body of his wife. Seventeen persons in this family which had
never known sorrow perished in that terrible catastrophe.

Also, a year later, the eldest daughter of Dillaye, who
had been separated from her mother, died of a kind of con-
sumption. Dillaye had to wait long before he could return to
his usual occupations.

Three months after my arrival, Léon Gaumont wanted very
much to accompany I know not what presidential voyage to
Algeria. He asked permission of Max Richard, who at first
refused. Current affairs demanded Gaumont's presence,
Richard said. Gaumont's disappointment was so sharp that
I gathered my courage to say to Max Richard: "Sir, I think
I am now au courant enough to take charge of the ordinary
correspondence for a few days. If something difficult arises
I could submit it to you when you pass by the office."

Léon Gaumont caught the ball on the bounce. "I am
certain that Mademoiselle Alice can manage affairs very well,"
he stated. "Besides, I'll be away for a week at most."

"Very well," said Richard, "let's hope all goes well."

Gaumont left, happy as a schoolboy on vacation. I had
the good luck that no important mistakes were made during
his voyage. I had, from that day, gained his complete confidence and maybe a little respect on the part of Max Richard.

My salary rose. Alas, so did my responsibilities. Bit
by bit, the reins of all the services were united in my hands:
opening, annotation, distribution of the mail, checking of
work, surveying the packing, the posting of orders, renewing
the stock. In the absence of the chiefs, I had contact with
the important clients. Finally, all correspondence, properly
speaking. Sometimes I felt discouragement come over me.
As soon as one task was accomplished another was added.
But the despondency was brief.

We had found under the roof of an ancient mansion,
quai Malaquais, facing the statue of Voltaire (him again) a
charming little apartment as bright as possible. From our
windows, lightly mansarded, we enjoyed an admirable view:
to the east the silhouette of Nôtre-Dame, in front of us Saint-

Germain l'Auxerrois, the Louvre, the Tuileries. To the west,
Sevres and Saint-Cloud in the distance. Under our eyes was
all the activity of the Seine, the barges, the small tradesmen
on the banks: dog shearers, clippers of cats, the bookstalls
along the quai, the water bearers. All that was gay and
lively.

I could hardly keep from laughing, when I met, on the
staircase, the Count of R. de S. burning sugar on a red-hot
fire-shovel in order to chase away...before the arrival of
guests...the odor of tripe and onions bubbling in the concierge's quarters.

Returning homeward I would stroll a bit. Crossing the
garden of the Tuileries, full of flowers, with beribboned
nursemaids, children, the bridge of Saints-Peres, the teasing
students (the School of Beaux-Arts was in our neighborhood),
these partly made me forget my worries.

I climbed joyfully up into our pigeonnier which my
mother, now freed from her worries, used all her ingenuity
to make comfortable and cheerful. She had used to the full-
est the few fine pieces of furniture and art objects remaining
from happier days. Old recipes permitted her to prepare excellent meals that my youthful appetite still seasons in memory.
Life seemed beautiful to me. Making my morning toilet I sang
aloud.

However, a great cloud rose on the horizon. Jules
Richard, inventor of the recording barometer and the stereo-
scope which bear his name, filed suit against his brother Max,
our director, to prohibit him from the manufacture of cameras.
He won this suit and the head of our company was obliged to
retire. This meant within a brief delay, the closure of the
shop and the discharge of employees. Léon Gaumont was
married, with three children; his anxiety was great, and my
own could let me guess at his.

But Léon Gaumont, Barbist [a student of the College of
Saint-Barbe in Paris], eager worker, had earned his stripes
as an engineer with Carpentier, the eminent builder of scientific instruments, especially binoculars, the sales of which he
trusted to Gaumont.

I had often noticed the special respect our principal
clients showed him.

"Why not," I asked "call on them to form a company which would allow you to continue?"

"I have thought of that," Gaumont told me. "I have spoken of it to a few of them who seemed interested."

Man of action that he was, he executed his project with energy. Several weeks later the Société en commandite Léon Gaumont et Cie was formed with a board of directors: Eiffel, Vallot, Viviani and other important members (among them, the Belgian consul whose name I forget) and affairs progressed well again.

On the lands his wife possessed at Belleville Gaumont built model factories for the manufacture of the cameras he had invented: spido, stereo-spido, etc., as well as a studio for the development and printing of photographic works, the numbers of which grew daily.

In the course of this year we received the visit of a very amiable and young savant, Georges Demeny, nervous, well-bred. His knowledge seemed unlimited: music, special mathematics, mechanics and physics, anatomy, he was a professor of physical education at the School of Arts et Métiers. He had touched on everything. He was lately associated with [Etienne-Jules] Marey, the physiologist, in the creation of a laboratory specially designed for the study of motion in humans and animals, and especially the flight of birds. Aviation was germinating.

Towards this end he had invented a camera which he baptized phonoscope which permitted the recording on a glass disc coated with emulsion of a series of images which, when projected, gave the illusion of movement and changing facial expression. This was the camera he proposed that Gaumont should exploit. I was present at the interview.

Gaumont was very interested. A company was formed to study the various patents held by Demeny.

The phonoscope had already received several transformations in order to create a camera capable of both recording and projecting motion pictures, when Gaumont received the visit of two old frineds, Auguste and Louis Lumière. They came to invite him to attend a meeting of the Société

d'encouragement à l'industrie nationale where the two brothers
would present a new camera of their invention. I was present
at the interview and they invited me, also, but they refused
to give us any explication of their instrument.

"You'll see," they said "it's a surprise."

Our curiosity was wakened. We were careful not the
miss the meeting.

A few days later [on December 28, 1895], the first
Lumière movie was given its first showing in the basement of
the Grand Café, 14 boulevard des Capucines.

There was great competition among producers. Gaumont
was very advanced in this race and came in a good second
with the chronophotographe. Unfortunately, he had chosen
to use 60 mm film which required certain changes and slowed
him at the start.

But Gaumont, like Lumière, was especially interested in
solving mechanical problems. It was one more camera to put
at the disposition of his clients. The educational and enter-
tainment values of motion pictures seemed not to have caught
his attention. Nevertheless, there had been created, in the
ruelle des Sonneries, a little laboratory for the development
and printing of short "shots": parades, railroad stations,
portraits of the laboratory personnel, which served as demonstration films but were both brief and repetitious.

Daughter of an editor, I had read a good deal and retained quite a bit. I had done a little amateur theatricals
and I thought that one might do better than these demonstration films. Gathering my courage, I timidly proposed to
Gaumont that I might write one or two little scenes and have
a few friends perform in them. If the future development of
motion pictures had been foreseen at this time, I should never
have obtained his consent.

My youth, my inexperience, my sex, all conspired
against me.

I did receive permission, however, on the express condition that this would not interfere with my secretarial duties.
I had to be in the office every morning at eight o'clock to

open, record and distribute the mail. Then I was free to take
the four-horse omnibus that, by the rue La Fayette, climbed
to the Buttes Chaumont, and use as well as I could the time
that remained to me. By 4:30 I had to be back at the rue
Saint-Roch office, to do the personal correspondence, get
signatures, etc. That often took until ten or eleven at night.
Finally then I would be free to return to the quai Malaquais
to take a few hours of rest, which I felt I really had earned.

It was at this epoch that Léon Gaumont, finding that
I lost too much time in going to and fro, offered to arrange
for me a little house he owned at the bottom of the ruelle des
Sonneries, behind the photographic studio, which he rented
to me for a minimal sum (eight hundred francs per year, all
the same). Seeing my hesitation, he promised to install a
bath and to have the garden cleared by a Buttes Chaumont
gardener. I ended by agreeing. I was already bitten by the
demon of the cinema.

It was not without regret that we left our pigeonnier on
the quai Malaquais. A rather low wall separated the lot of
the new lodging from a little island inhabited by the slaughter-
house workers of La Villette. Shortly after we had moved,
heart-rending cries drew me to a window. One of our good
neighbors returning from work had found his wife and daughter on the ground before a litre of wine intended for him,
which the little girl had dropped. Drunk with rage, he wound
the woman's hair around his fist and, with all his force, struck
her head against the bricks of their house. I refused to endure this for long. Besides, these neighborhoods disquieted
Gaumont also and he first heightened the wall and then later
bought the whole complex.

Thus I became acquainted with my new domain. It was in
this garden that we planted, Anatole [Thiberville] and I, our
first film camera.

In 1896 unions did not exist. The work-week was six
days, sometimes seven, hours of work...unlimited. I remember
a Sunday morning when Gaumont came to ask me to run
around the garden, in order to measure the speed of the
course, thanks to a camera of his invention. This I repeat,
is what is called today "la belle époque."

At Belleville, next to the photographic laboratories, I

was given an unused terrace with an asphalt floor (which
made it impossible to set up a real scene) and a shaky glass
ceiling, overlooking a vacant lot. It was in this palace that
I made my first efforts. A backdrop painted by a fan-painter
(and fantasist) from the neighborhood made a vague decor,
with rows of wooden cabbages cut out by a carpenter, costumes rented here and there around the Porte Saint-Martin.
As actors: my friends, a screaming baby, an anxious mother
leaping to and fro into the camera focus, and my first film
La Fée Aux choux was born. Today it is a classic of which
the Cinémathèque français preserves the negative.*

I should exaggerate if I told you it was a masterpiece,
but the public then was not jaded, the actors were young and
pleasing, and the film had enough success that I was allowed
to try again.

It was there, thanks to the good will of my little acting
troupe, and the advice and lessons of Frederic Dillaye (technical adviser to the Gaumont establishment and author of excellent books on art photography), to the experience gained
day by day, to luck, that we discovered many little tricks
such as:

Films turned in reverse, permitting one to take a house
falling down and then reconstructed as if by magic;

A person falling from a roof and jumping up spontanta-
neously;

A greedy client at the bakery, finding his bill to high,
giving back intact the swallowed cakes.

Films slowed down or accelerated by a turn of the
handle, transforming peaceful passersby into creatures seized
by frenzy or, on the contrary, sleepwalking.

---

*It is the opinion of French film historian Francis Lacassin
that La Fée aux choux dates from 1900, not 1896. The basis
for this opinion is that the film bears the number 397 in the
Gaumont catalog and appears immediately before an actuality
short which can accurately be dated August-September 1900.

Stops, permitting one to displace an object which in projection would seem to be animated by a supernatural life, stupefying an archeologist when his precious mummy plays in the laboratory. Example: La Momie.*

Double exposures.

Fade-outs used for visions and dreams.

We also made some films outdoors. Having discovered, during a walk in Barbizon, an old coach, I decided to use it to represent the mail-coach from Lyon.** A professional troupe would have been too costly, but I persuaded our own personnel to replace them.

Supplied with a copious home-made lunch, costumes and necessary accessories, almost all of us with bicycles, we took the train as far as Melun. At the station two or three carriages, whose drivers called themselves guides to the forest of Fontainebleau, took the baggage and the less sportive young ladies and we rolled towards Barbizon where the stage waited for us.

Then the guides led us to a site they thought suitable. There, after having wolfed the picnic, we distributed the costumes. The ladies hid as well as they could behind the bushes; the men, less prudish, dressed themselves anywhere. Happily the forest was empty as we must have made an odd spectacle.

In spite of the autumn coolness the enterprise was a success. Gaiety and good humor went with us, and we promised ourselves that we'd repeat the experience.

All these very short films (seventeen or twenty-five metres in length) taken in unbelievable conditions, contained the germ of today's creations.

In Cinema Total, Essai sur les formes futures du cinema [Editions Denoël, Paris, 1944], René Barjavel tells us, "The silent cinema was as lovely as a child playing in the sunshine

---

*This film remains unidentified.
**Produced as L'Assassinat du Courrier de Lyon, April 1904.

but...when young people of our time have occasion to see a
film retrospective, they find them rather grotesque and are
surprised by the sadness of their elders."

My impression is different. In the silent cinema, we
had discovered a fresh, limpid spring, joyously reflecting the
grasses, watercress and willows that bordered it; we had only
to wet our lips in it to staunch our thirst. Its prattle murmured of things, no doubt childish, which she pressed us to
repeat in our turn, first message to those whom she could not
reach and refresh.

Our spring has followed its course, swollen by currents
less pure. It has become a rivulet, then a river, has crossed
great cities which dirtied it with their gutters. From every
corner of the world gold hunters have arrived. They have
stirred this mud, now we smell its fetid odors. They have
sown the seed of poison flowers which now trim our altars.
God willing, perhaps science, so powerful today, will succeed
in purifying all that. Let us not wonder at the melancholy
of the young. Enough romanticism; let us return to reality.

I would not have, I think, any pleasure in seeing one
of my first films. My readers, if I have any, must consider
the conditions in which we worked. The early cameras, with
their outside reel-cases, ill adjusted, the methods of drawing
the film not yet mastered, the tripods which were the same
as those employed in still photography and which sank in the
soft earth of our garden giving them something less than
stability. We had the use of only one focus, the traction of
the reel was accomplished by an outside crank turned by
hand. The frame, trimmed with velvet, retained the dust
which scratched the emulsion.

My faithful cameraman Anatole Thiberville (who, before
becoming a cinematographer raised chickens in Bresse, if I
remember) helped me with endless patience and good will.
I have kept an excellent memory of him.

The other film producers who sprang up concurrently
used our discoveries as soon as we made them. [Ferdinand]
Zecca, the only contributor, who stayed about two weeks with
me before joining Pathé, filmed Les Méfaits d'une tête de veau
[1904] (film falsely attributed later to me). It was interesting
because it illustrated the method of stoppages, during which
one displaced objects, as in La Momie.

During the projection of films in the rue Saint-Roch, the reactions of some of the clients were amusing. I have seen some who, suspecting some trick, went behind the screen to see if we didn't have accomplices acting out the scene.

CHAPTER FOUR

It was also on this little terrace [at Belleville] that we made the first effort at talking pictures, the "chronophone."* The songs and music were recorded in the studios on a cylinder of wax. It was there that I filmed the director of the Opéra Gaillard who came to see me with the ballet mistress and a group of dancers to whom he himself gave a lesson in triple battement de pieds (I think that's the term). He was then more than seventy years old.

It is easy to record on the wax cylinder. That ease cost me some of the most embarrassing moments of my life.

Once a week, my mother and I went to spend an evening at the house of friends in the faubourg Saint-Germain, a very agreeable environment but very formal. Knowing that we were making these recordings, our friends asked us to bring an instrument and some cylinders, among others, the "Ave Maria" of Gounod [La Prière]. In the attentive silence the first part of the "Ave Maria" played without incident, but with all the faults of the early efforts. The end came and I was going to take the needle from the last groove; someone interrupted me, saying "Wait, there's still something." I obeyed, unhappily, and in the deep silence a masculine voice rose offering these words: "Oh! The cad, he has a hairy a...." A still deeper silence followed these last words and I felt myself go pale and then blush. But when I lifted my eyes, the dismayed faces of the audience worked such a reaction on me that I was taken by irrepressible giggles which infected the listeners. I promised myself to examine the cylinders in the future before playing them in public. You will recognize, I think, the spirit of the Parisian worker.

---

*Of which Alice Guy made more than 100 between 1900 and 1907.

At the end of a year and a half or two years, the success proved such, and the profits were so substantial, that
the Board of Directors decided to build a studio [in the Buttes
Chaumont in 1905].

This period was hard for me. I had been left to work
out alone the difficulties at the beginning, to break new
ground, but when the affair became interesting, doubtless
lucrative, my directorship was bitterly disputed. However,
I was combative and thanks to president [Gustave] Eiffel,
who always encouraged me with kindness, the whole Board of
Directors, recognizing my efforts, decided to leave me at the
head of the service. Apparently there was nothing to complain of, since in spite of the underground war waged against
me by the director of the production workshops [René Decaux],
and in spite of the ill-temper that led him to commit a thousand pettinesses...not only against me but also against the
employees who worked under my orders...I succeeded in keeping my post until 1907, that is to say for eleven years.

Happily not all the engineers were so hostile. I could
only congratulate myself on my relations with [P.] Frely, who
worked on talking pictures; Laudet, who perfected the sound
amplifiers; Santou, who invented the mechanical developer.
They never refused me their counsel and helped me to the
best of their ability with any troublesome problem.

To return to the studio, as Gaumont and Company never
did things by halves, they decided to take the stage of the
Opera as model, with all the Opera's underpinnings, flying
bridges, trapdoors, slanted floor-boards, all things which
were not only useless but harmful. Next to this stage, an
enormous glass cage, freezing in winter, burning in summer,
completed our new domain. To remedy the frequent absence
of sunlight, two heavy scaffolds had been constructed sup-
porting twenty-four lamps of thirty amperes, which caused
us bad electric insolation. I have passed so many nights
half blind, with weeping eyes unable to read. Many of the
actors had the same experience and attacked the Company,
obliging them to change the lighting. Personally I have still
a retraction of the retina, sometimes very troubling. Finally,
an enormous industrial smokestack threw its shadow over our
stage every morning.

The public that laughs at these early productions, the

stage directors who profit today from the progress based on
our efforts and research, certainly do not take account of
our difficulties.

Our little films of seventeen metres, then twenty-five
metres, were developed, fixed, dried by hand. Rolled on
wooden frames, they were placed in vertical tanks containing
the chemical baths of hydroquinone, métol, etc. which an employee was then charged with agitating constantly to avoid
that these salts resting on the film should make irregular
zones of light. Too hot a bath would riddle the film with
little holes. Often the film detached itself from the frame,
like an onion skin, rendering a whole day's work useless.
One had to be patient, begin again, persevere. But the staff
was good, as I said, and we did our work gaily.

Many of our films were colored. Two workers, installed
at tables equipped for them like those that serve today for
montage, jewelers' glass at eye, would comb with fine brushes
and transparent colors the images in which the actors were
lilliputian. Imagine the care and patience necessary for this
work when one considers the enlargement these images sus-
tained upon projection. This early procedure was followed by
that of cutting three ribbons to serve as stencils for mechanical coloration. This decoupage was made with the aid of a
cutting pen, "le stedik," and required the same care, the
same dexterity as that earlier process.

I regret not remembering the names of those workers.
They surely merited listing as collaboraters in the early
phase.

The first outdoor films, in the streets of Paris, were
trials to us. We did not have specially equipped automobiles,
as we might today. One or two fiacres carried us, my actors,
Anatole and myself, to the chosen location. Hardly had we
placed our camera and given some directions to the actors
when we were surrounded by idle onlookers. They took
great interest in the camera, and often while Anatole was
under his black photographer's drape, trying to focus, he
would find himself face to face with a gaper. Or a busybody
on her way to market would cross the camera, loudly inquir-
ing as to these clowns who burdened the sidewalk. Then
would come the police, capes waving, shouting "Circulate!
Circulate!" Happily, the chief of police at that time, M. Lepine,

to whom I recounted my adventures, armed me with a permit
that not only ordered people to let me work in peace, but
also to help me as much as possible.

The studio being finished, I took possession and left
my asphalt terrace without regret. The first film that I produced, La Esmeralda [1905], was the last flare of our fan-
painter. Coming on the stage I stopped perplexed. The
decor represented a corner of old Paris, all right, but my
painter was certainly a Futurist. The lop-sided houses were
ringed with corkscrew spirals right up under their pointed
bonnets. The goat that I had tried to tame during a whole
week followed me faithfully, refusing the company of Esmeralda. Mounted on the torture rack, the unhappy Quasimodo
tried to steady the balls of cotton with which be had stuffed
his costume for realism, but they moved in all directions,
turning the drama to farce...the torture was mine!

There could be no question of beginning over, the
overall costs were running up and when the cost of a film
passed ten thousand francs I would be summoned by the
Board of Directors and asked if I intended to ruin the company!...You are familiar with the costs of film production today, but I repeat, these were gold francs.

Monsieur [Georges] Sadoul, author of a history of the
cinema from those heroic times...who, misled, and doubtless
in all good faith (he says himself that he is ignorant of that
epoch and speaks only from hearsay), has attributed my first
films to people who probably worked for the Gaumont studios
only as actors, whose names I don't even know...has unin-
tentionally paid me great compliments concerning La Esmeralda.

We had bought some used theatre curtains at Belleville
or at the Saint-Martin gate. Profiting from one of the cut-
out doorways I had lowered behind the opening one of the   ·
curtains representing a faraway town. The effect was rather
good and M. Sadoul declares that it was a very original and
happy novelty.

I had the occasion to meet M. Sadoul and to show him
the documents which persuaded him that the films in question
were my work. He promised me to rectify this passage in
his next editions, which he faithfully did, although his num-
bering still contains errors. La Fée aux choux dates from

1896; the following from 1897-1898, <u>Les Petits Coupeurs du bois vert</u>; Déménagement a la cloche de bois; <u>Volée par les Bohémiens</u>; <u>Le Matelas</u>. Besides, I am giving the exact list and the dates, certified by the postcards printed at that epoch by the Gaumont Company.*

Until then I had worked alone. After a few months I was given two assistants of whom one, [Louis] Feuillade, shines in the first rank in the list of early animators, a secretary, Yvonne Serand, who had acted in <u>La Fée aux choux</u> and later became the wife of the director Arnaud who directed several comic films, and finally, [Henri] Menessier the set-designer whose collaboration was precious to me and who rejoined me in the United States.

Every Monday we discussed the week's work together. The studio became a hive of activity. Thus we made a series of comic films, pursuits, tumbles, clashes, acrobatics, what one calls "slapstick." The extras were usually provided by the personnel of the workshops.

However, we had engaged a casting director, Denizot. He introduced into the studio such wordly contacts as made me understand how ignorant I was of the range of human types.

One day Denizot had led in some extras who would appear in tights in some fairy-tale. On the stage, Gaumont discussed some technical detail. They called me over to discuss the matter. At that moment, one of the women left the dressing room, in the most simple attire...her tights over her arm.

"I am so sorry, Mademoiselle," she said, "I'm in my bad days and have spotted your tights."

I felt myself blush. The men turned discreetly away, no doubt smiling at my embarrassment. I hardened quickly.

However, other companies were formed and the extras they employed irregularly came to offer us their services.

---

*These postcards were donated to the Cinémathèque Française of Henri Langlois and are now "lost."

We would engage them and they, naturally, would then hurry
to tell our competitors about our activities.

It was thus that La Guérite appeared simultaneously in
the catalogues of both Gaumont and Pathé. When I protested
to the latter company I was answered that this was fair war-
fare and we had only to do the same.

From this epoch dates:

Le Chapeau* by [Etienne] Arnaud, I think. A hat,
which was blown on the roof, rolls down slanted streets, is
blown through a coal cellar, always followed by its unhappy
owner. Also, Thé chez la concierge, C'est Papa qui prend la
purge, and some others.

At about the same time I engaged a troupe of English
acrobats, the O'Mers, with whom I had great pleasure working. Young, full of enthusiasm, gaiety, courage, they accepted the most thankless roles. Together we made, among
other things, Une Noce a Robinson** about donkeys, with
acrobats in the trees; A la réchérche d'un appartement, in
which the floor crumbled, and the chandelier fell down; Le
Départ pour les vacances with impossible valises, and an iras-
cible driver of a fiacre which fell to pieces; Le Démenagement
á la cloche de bois with its ruses for putting the concierge
off the track, and its unstable furniture.

Finally, La Mariée du lac Saint-Fargeau [Une Noce au
lac Saint-Fargeau], a film inspired by a tale of Paul de Kock.

I don't know if the lake still exists. It was not far
from the studio, at the top of the rue de Belleville, the remains of a splendid property which had belonged to Michel
le Peletier, lord of Saint-Fargeau who had built a castle
there. Under Louis XV the property belonged, it appears,
to Madame de Pompadour. Some lilac bushes surrounded a
little lake, last of these splendors.

A cheap restaurateur had installed some little tables
around the waterpiece, for Sunday picnickers. One might,

---

*Attrapez mon chapeau or Le coup du vent, both from 1904.
**An unidentified film.

said a poster, bring one's own food, but the proprietor also
served mussels and the fried potatoes popular at all the gates
of Paris.

It was from him that I ordered a prepared meal. We
found, on our arrival, a long table placed between the lake
and a swing suspended from a little portal buried in lilacs.
A property-man could not have done better. The wedding
party arrived: bitter mother-in-law, father-in-law already a
little tipsy, odd guests preceded by a whimpering bride and
her bridegroom. Everyone settled down, intending to enjoy
the occasion. But the bride (in the performance, the young-
est of the O'Mer family) had noticed the swing and insisted on
trying it. The best man thought it was his duty to satisfy
her and, proud of his muscles, gave the swing such a shove
that the young woman, torn from her seat, made an arc
over the table and was precipitated into the little lake.

All the wedding party jumped to her aid. But I was
seized with horror and remorse when the actress came out of
that cesspool. She was covered up to her hair with fetid,
blackish mud, crawling with larvae. For how long a time had
that lake not been cared for! However, when the disaster
was repaired, I heard neither complaint nor reproach and
everyone took up the work again with the same enthusiasm.

When they left me for a world tour, they sent me post-
cards with their best wishes, for a long time after.

Searching for a setting for a film La Pègre de Paris I
walked along a part of the old fortifications which still existed
in those days. A mattress-maker had installed her frame for
stretching the canvas. She finished filling it with wool which
she had just carded. For I know not what reason, she left
her work and went away for a few minutes. Almost at once
a drunk arrived, climbed the mound and rested in contempla-
tion before the half-finished mattress.

This little tableau suggested the idea for a film [Matelas
alcoolique, 1906] which later had a great success. Here is
the scenario:

"Some days before his marriage, a young man left his
mattress with a mattress-maker who promised to put it in excellent shape before the wedding night."

I reconstructed the scene I had witnessed but in my story,

> the wine-loving drunk really lay down in the bed and was completely buried. The mattress-maker, unsuspecting, returned and finished her work. A porter arrived, loaded the mattress on his cart and left in haste. The drunk, half-wakened, stirred, upsetting the balance and there was a series of tumbles down the stairways of Montmartre, across a little bridge, near a wash-house, into a urinal, etc., always followed by the unfortunate porter.
>
> The young couple waited impatiently for the mattress. Finally, it arrived. The exhausted porter flung the mattress on the bed-spring, pocketed his tip and fled.
>
> In haste, the newlyweds made the bed and prepared to pass an agreeable night. The drunk inconvenienced, began a series of jumps. The distracted couple cried for help. The police of that era came running and led the lovers and the mattress to the police station. All was finally explained and the drunk went to finish his nap in a cell.

Our first clients, the Grenier family, circus owners, invited me to Rouen to help in the projection of the Matelas alcoolique in their theatre. As I have just told you, I had personally directed it.

This was a holiday for me. I did not know any circus showmen. The Greniers came to meet me at the station in one of the first autos, painted red and bearing their name in golden latters. They possessed ten or so rolling vans as clean and comfortable as the best American trailer. Everyone in this family of seven or eight children had his employment: the father and eldest son took care of the projection, the mother was cashier, the daughters played in the intermission, etc.

The projections took place in a great tent like a circus. I took a seat in the audience and heard an explosion of gaiety that may be rarely surpassed at Cluny or at the Palais-Royal. In front of me, one young woman twisted in her chair and begged between shouts of laughter: "Enough, enough, I'll make pipi."

After the showing, the Grenier family presented me to
their public and gave me a superb sheaf of roses and a fine
pedigreed dog. This was my first encounter with Fame. I
hope some member of the family will read these lines and find
here how gratefully I remember them.

At that epoch we paid no attention to copyright and
sought our inspiration just about everywhere. Personally,
I was inspired:

By two Grand Guignol plays for L'Asile de nuit; Le
Paralytique; Lui; Au Téléphone.
By some Guillaume drawings for Amoureux transis;
Professeur de langues vivantes (concerning this film,
Gaumont asked me sternly how I happened to know that
milieu); La Fève enchantée.
By various plays, legends, novels for Lèvres closes;
La Légende de Saint-Nicolas; Conscience de prêtre.

However, there were daily improvements. The film itself, thanks to Planchon, a co-worker of Lumière, was much
longer and of better quality. One of our engineers, Santou,
created the first system of automatic development replacing
the inconveniences of developing the film by hand, and permitting the development, fixing, and drying of films of unlimited length. The cinema camera was made more stable,
more tight. The series of big films began, as well as long
documentaries.

Gaumont himself accompanied the presidents Félix Faure
and Loubet on their respective trips to Russia and Africa.
He did not at all like to be reminded of the short periods in
his life when he had personally carried the camera on his
shoulder, considering them as the sins of his youth.

Thanks to the automatic development process of Santou,
Le Delhi Durbar, Le premier vol de Santos-Dumont, and La
première course Paris-Marseille (in which one of the Renault
brothers died) were filmed by our workers and were projected
twenty-four or forty-eight hours after filming.

At the Exposition of 1900 the projection of our films
constituted one of the principal attractions.

The Compagnie des Wagons-Lits had asked the Gaumont

company to send its operators on board the Trans-Siberian Railway to make a documentary of the countryside, forests, along the course of that line. The film was projected by the decorater Jambon in a Paris street reconstructed after his models for this Exposition.

I remember my meeting with Jambon, at that time a decorater celebrated for his scenes of Paris. Gaumont being absent, I received him and very naturally put myself entirely at his disposition for all the information that he needed. He was grateful and we became a pair of friends. When I went to see him in the vast workshop he possessed near the Buttes Chaumont, to order some scenery curtains from him, there were twenty or so painters working on canvases stretched out on the ground. Jambon flung out his absurd order, which terribly tried my shyness, "To arms, gentlemen! Here is the Princess!" and all the daubers hurried to place their long brushes on their shoulders.

Science was not absent from our activities.

Personally, I have often aided Doctor François-Franck of the Institute when he was studying, with the aid of the cinema, the respiration process compared in humans and animals, the heart-beats of a dog during vivisection, the movement of paralytics, the different facial expressions of the mad.

At the headquarters of Gaumont Co., Rue Saint-Roch, clients pressed to see the first x-ray (Roentgen ray) experiments with reels by (I think) Carpentier, which permitted one to see the skeleton through the flesh, and for which I have often lent my hands, without suspecting any danger. I still have a little burn scar from this.

The Gaumont establishment also took films of the experiments of Cailletet (compressed air), Monnier (studies of bees), of the Prince of Monaco (his oceanography museum) and others whom I have already cited.

Color film, after the methods of Ducos du Hauron and Lippmann, was in the study stage. It was finally achieved in 1912 and presented at the Gaumont Theatre, Boulevard Poissonniere. While waiting, we continued to color the film by stencil, and also to tint it night blue or sunlight yellow according to the atmosphere desired.

The role of director was complex: scenario, choice of actors, agreements with the decorators, the costumers, the furnishers. Finally, rehearsal, stage direction, lighting. Editing, cutting and montage of the finished film was also important.

I was fortunately seconded by excellent assistants of whom I have already spoken, and finally, in 1905 (two years before my departure for the United States) by Victorin Jasset, an artist who had staged the great processions in Jeanne d'Arc and in Vercingétorix at the Hippodrome before that enormous auditorium became the Gaumont Palace.

All did not go without a hitch. I had surprised the casting director, Vincent Denizot, bullying one of the men and I had threatened him with dismissal if the thing happened again. Encouraged, one of the poor devils came to me and confided that, from their meagre salary (at that juncture, three to five francs) this individual retained fifty centimes and delivered blows if they grumbled. To put an end to this abuse, I resolved to pay them myself. This did not suit the casting director, and he let me know it.

Having learned that a gipsy camp had settled near the still-extant Paris fortifications, I decided to use it as a setting for one of my scenarios Volée par les bohemiens. At the moment of starting out, I found on my desk an anonymous note warning me that someone was going to make me "lose my taste for meddling in affairs that didn't concern me." I was not very troubled. I had with me my cameraman, my actors, the animal-trainer Juliano who tamed a bear and who, though he had only one arm, was nevertheless quite husky.

The scene answered my expectations: wagons, swarthy men and women in dirty but colorful rags, outdoor kitchen, half-clothed kids frolicking with the goats and chickens.

Juliano had tied his bear under a wagon. The animal pulling on his chain succeeded in sniffing the heels of a starlet seated on the wagon steps and who, feeling the bear's muzzle, fled shrieking. The bear, excited by the environment, succeeded in escaping and jumped on a goat. That was a fine hubbub: the gipsies rushing to save their goat, Juliano pulling on the bear. The bear withdrew, but so brusquely that Juliano tumbled. Before he could get up again, the bear

jumped on an unfortunate little donkey who fled with wild
braying toward the city walls. That was a magnificent pursuit which Anatole had the coolness to photograph and which
added greatly to the interest of the film. The day finished
without further upsets. The gipsy chief, however, invited
me to go alone into his wagon in order to pay him. I declined, and seeing my staff approaching, he did not insist.
Had he been paid to frighten me?...it's quite possible.

To stage a drama about mining, inspired by a novel of
Zola's Jasset, my assistant, had suggested Fumay [where he
was born] a sad, dark little village of the Ardennes, reflected
in the Meuse. The main shaft was said to be in disrepair; I
had, to the great amusement of the miners, to dress up in a
miner's overalls and be lowered in a bucket for the five or
six hundred metres underground by the narrow passageway
now serving as a shaft. The lower galleries, shored up by
timbering which seemed insufficient to me, had enormous
slabs of slate shaken down by explosions, which the engineers
surveyed minutely, studying the slide with the aid of melted
wax poured between the blades of slate. All that seemed
threatening enough to me. I felt, I admit, a certain relief
to find myself again in the fresh air, but happy for this new
experience, this enrichment.

At that time there were dog-carts transporting the milk,
inhabitants in regional dress, the Belgian customs-officers,
who provided us with excellent material. We had, unfortunately, to regret two rather grave accidents: a child knocked
down by the dogs; an extra who took a bad fall. My actors
were superstitious, like all theatre people, and attributed
these accidents to an unhappy salamander taken from the
woods, which I wanted to take back to Doctor François-Franck
for his studies. To crown the bad luck, during the night
the poor little beast gave birth to seven little salamanders.
At the moment of getting into the train, myself carrying the
precious salamander and her little ones, I was a bit jostled,
the jar got away from me and rolled under the train, which
started up, and everyone breathed again.

Many people who have never set foot in a studio before
1930...and perhaps even since then...believe that we used
to work without scenarios. Nothing could be more false. Except for the very earliest films of twenty or twenty-five metres everything was prepared in advance: the story written

with care, the cast, decor, the costumes prepared in detail
and distributed at each shooting. Otherwise, how could we
have avoided going down in disorder?...Even if we didn't
have a script-girl.

Competition was hard. We were protected by no laws.
The extras, employed indifferently by all the studios, served
as spies, which obliged us to race to finish first.

I had long wanted to make a film about the fine drama
of the Passion. At the 1900 Exposition, Tissot had published
a very beautiful Bible illustrated after the sketches he had
made in the Holy Land. It was ideal documentation, for decors, costumes and even local customs. I bought that Bible,
which I still have. Jasset was primarily useful for filming
the outside scenes and in the administration of three hundred
extras. I undertook to put my project to execution.

Menessier, of whom I have already spoken, and Garnier,
son of the constructor of the Opera, another excellent decorator who succeeded him, built twenty-five solid sets, an
enormous number for that epoch.

This was for the director of the studios [René Decaux]
one more occasion to evidence his desire to collaborate in our
success. The winter was very cold, and fearing, he said,
that the pipes should burst, he availed himself one night of
the scenery flats already built by the set shops and had them
sawed up in order to insulate the pipes. This cost us only
ten days or so of delay, as the disgusted employees sincerely
wanted to make up for this action.

The actors were chosen with care. We had to give a
hand in preparing the costumes. Two Jesuits, the Fathers
Chevalier and X..., returning from Palestine, attended the
filming and helped us with their counsels. Some of the scenes
required numerous extras, up to 250 or even 300 persons,
an important number for that time.

The exterior shots were taken in the forest of Fontainebleau, even though there were no olive trees there, as we
were learning to take just part of a beautiful landscape, filmed against the light, with a ray of sunshine filtering through
the trees. The Angel presenting the Chalice to Our Lord,
the climb up Calvary, the Entombment, all these scenes

succeeded. Jesus rising from the Sepulchre was one of our
best superimpositions. This was one of the first big spectacle films and I had the honor, very rare at that period, of
being named as director when the film was presented at the
Société de photographie de Paris, as the bulletin of that
showing can witness. Happily for me, as many persons tried
to take credit for that work.*

Certain authors of works on the debuts of the cinema
state that we took only very short films. But La Passion,
filmed in the first months of 1906, measured 600 metres and
contained twenty-five solidly constructed sets, a cast of two
or three hundred persons for each of whom we had, with my
assistant Jasset, to drape each costume after the documents
in the work of Tissot.

It was thanks to Planchon, one of the collaborators with
Lumière, who first found the means to manufacture very long
strips of celluloid, and to Santou, who invented the apparatus
for mechanical development, fixing and drying of films, that
it was possible at that epoch to obtain films of an appreciable
length.

---

*Presumably a reference to Georges Sadoul's crediting the
film -- known as La Vie du Christ, La Passion, La Vie de
Jesus or La Passion de Christ -- to "Jasset...with the as-
sistance of Georges Hatot."

CHAPTER FIVE

In his memoirs, Léon Gaumont says that after obtaining the first film he was obsessed by the desire to give the images sound, color, and depth. This was the chronophone, first talking picture, a French invention.

Thanks to the engineers already cited, the first talking film, this time on a disc, was achieved in 1900.

It was not the talking picture as you know it. The voice of the artist (singer, speaker), the music for the dance were recorded in the studio. The actors then rehearsed their roles until they had obtained a perfect synchronization with the phonographic recording. Then the cinematographic record was taken. The two instruments (photo and phono) were united by an electric contrivance which assured their synchronization.

I was charged with the cinematographic part of the repertoire and thus filmed the Mante sisters, very fashionable popular dancers at that time; Rose Caron of the Opéra, with her singing class. With Mme Mathieu-Luce and Marguerite Care of the Opéra-Comique, Noté of the Opéra, Mlle Bourgois and others, we recorded Faust, Mignon, Carmen, Les Dragons de Villars, Mireille and many others. The Café-Concert itself was made to contribute, with Mayol, Dranem, Polin, Fragson and many others.

I have often been forced to admire the courage of the artists and their professional loyalty. Two anecdotes will make you appreciate these qualities. Mme Mathieu-Luce was singing the air from Mignon "Connais-tu le pays." She went straight to the end, smiling, but when the camera stopped, she fainted. She had placed her bare foot on a burning ember fallen from an arc lamp, and endured the burn rather than interrupt the filming.

I have had the same experience with the O'Mers, the company of English clowns of whom I told you. In jumping through a fake window, the chief acrobat tore the nails from one hand, but did not pause for so small a concern....

Famous artists, those whom I call the great artists, have not always inspired the same esteem in me. Today it is considered good fortune to act on the screen. Well-known authors, who have mocked at this art, are now only too happy to draw appreciable benefits from it. But at the time, they professed for the cinema, of which they understood nothing, scorn and extreme ill-will.

Camille Blanc, director of the Monte Carlo casino, often employed a celebrated Italian tenor, Caruso, no less. He proposed that we should record some chronophonic scenes with this artist. We made an appointment with Caruso and it was agreed that he should sing several of his successes for us, of which he furnished us the titles.

The date was set. The sets discussed, as well as the extras, etc. To do him honor, I entrusted the sets (at that moment ten back-drops) to a well-known and very expensive decorator, Jambon, of whom I have already spoken.

On the agreed date, I sent one of my assistants to find the great star in one of the company's first automobiles (a Panhard and Levassor), but he answered that he had thought it over and that with his name, he could not reasonably be expected to demean himself to this degree. Which proves that a good voice is not always the sign of an excellent education.

However, how many artists have gained by seeing themselves on the screen? How often I've heard the phrase "That's me, that one? I did this? But it's so bad. I beg you, let's do that over...."

That's because the camera is pitiless, revealing the least mannerism, underlining affectation. If the modern theatre has evolved towards more sobriety, more truth, I am persuaded that this is owed in great part to the cinema. Consequently, everywhere in my United States studio, there were posters "Be natural." During a visit he made me, a secretary of the Comedie-Française, Paul Capellani, remarked at these posters with a smile a bit ironic.

"Do your actors conform to your wishes?" he asked.

"Certainly, they try."

"You're lucky. Personally, it took me eleven years to reach this goal."

"Our technique is different...and on the screen they see themselves, judge themselves, and if they are intelligent they profit by the lesson to which I add my comments."

The chronophone gave me the occasion for an unforgettable journey in Spain. It was my enemy, the director of workshops, who procured this joy for me, involuntarily. He insisted that Gaumont should let him, himself, make the cinematographic record of a series of discs. Gaumont conceded, and in order to give him a free hand, he asked me to go, myself, with my camera-man Anatole as usual to take some sound pictures in Spain, where we had a branch and numerous clients. I accepted joyfully. The director of our affiliate in Barcelona had a charming wife who extended hospitality to me for several days. One of our clients, "Napoleon," who had met me in Paris which he visited frequently, had prepared a grandiose reception for me. I was, thanks to him, received on board a warship where the officers, after having offered me refreshments, led me on a tour of their ship and invited me to their table where a superb bouquet of camellias awaited me.

After visiting the city, very fine but rather banal with its houses too modern, too rich, with rectilinear avenues and shade-trees still too young, we made the famous pilgrimage up Montserrat. Many Spanish pilgrims climb on their knees, up the mountainous road cut by stations of the cross, leading to the Benedictine monastery where one finds the miraculous Virgin of the "nuevos," the newlyweds. Since the marriage of Isabelle the Catholic with Ferdinand II of Aragon, it seems that all Spanish sovereigns have held it a point of honor to provide this Virgin with sumptuous raiment. The day of our visit she wore a golden diadem glittering with precious stones, a cloak entirely embroidered with true pearls and a little handkerchief of real lace. The site itself was very fine. Anatole took many shots of it.

We left, then, for Saragossa where the men wear a

costume almost identical with that of cowboys. During our
overly short stay, I went early to stand at one end of the
bridge which crosses the Ebre, to watch the women, in their
bright costumes, perched on the little donkeys flanked with
two enormous jars of milk which they carry to market. The
men follow, dressed in leather pants trimmed with a cut
fringe, belt enhanced with big metal buttons, wide-brimmed
hat, living replicas of the Far West.

The people of Saragossa have kept a lively dislike for
the French, in memory of the Napoleonic wars.

They have a deep veneration for the Virgin of the Pil-
lar. Her statue is surrounded by ex-votos in colored wax,
so realistic that it is sometimes embarrassing to look at them.

Finally, they have a love of the dance. Their dancing
cost me one of the rare moments of ill-humor of my good
Anatole, when I insisted that evening on entering a cabaret
reserved for men. In passing, I had noticed a small stage
on which six guitar-players were seated. It was too tempt-
ing. While we descended the three steps leading to the room,
dark eyes watched me from under the sombreros. The cigar
smoke seemed to lift at faster intervals but that was all.
Soon the guitars introduced the dancer, who leaped forward,
castanets in her fingers. I did not regret my evening. Her
talent, grace and beauty would have conquered Paris at once.

Then there was Madrid. Madrid, la Puerta del Sol,
gate of the sun, so well-named. Its insolent toreadors, little
braid rolled at the nape, eying the señoritas and thrusting
out the chest, or capering about on Sunday before the bullfight. There was the fine Prado Museum, where the amusing
Infant and Infanta of Velasquez, paralysed by etiquette, contrast with the voluptuous Rubens and the diabolic Goya.

I had been recommended to the Master of the Queen's
Chapel. He spoke only a few words of French and I had forgotten quite a bit of my Spanish. He agreed, however, to
serve as guide and to show me the areas generally closed to
strangers. He led me to visit the Queen's Chapel where the
sovereign attended Mass in a loge closed by a great mirror.
The Oratory was somber, gloomy.

That evening he escorted me to a dance school where,

he said, we could expect to find dancers for our talking
films. We arrived rather late and I had a strange feeling.
The dancing master, a little Andalusian, introduced us into
a hall with walls entirely covered with mirrors. The uphol-
stered chairs were covered in red velvet. On the table decorated with a fine carpet were scattered the peelings of
shrimp. The Master had us sit, and set in our hands curious
drinking glasses with rounded bottoms, so that they could
not be set down. He filled these to the brim with sherry.
"Excuse me," he said "It's a little late, and my ballerinas
have already retired. However I'm going to call one."

He opened a door and called several times. After a
fairly long wait the "ballerina" made her entrance. It was a
poor little girl of twelve or so, who batted her eyelids ener-
getically to chase away sleep and yawned in a disturbing way.

The Master was upset, looking under the furniture,
murmuring "Donde esta mi sombrero?"...where is my hat?...
The search was in vain, he seized a cushon; "Bah!" said he
"this will do the job." He knelt on one knee and began to
whistle a bolero, then throwing the cushion in the direction
of the little girl, he clapped his hands rhythmically while the
poor child twirled as best she could. We signalled a quick
end to her trial. It was agreed that our host would wait for
us next day at a certain hacienda, a dance-hall on the banks
of the Manzanares, with a dozen of his best pupils. He kept
his word.

Very early the next day, we were at the meeting-place.
It was only to attend a fine fight. One of the big flower-
embroidered shawls which Spanish women like to wear was
missing. Two of the dancers seized one another by the hair
and, all claws out, disputed for the remaining one. I stopped
the combat by sending out to find another shawl and by
ordering the dancers to be served, while waiting, with the
thick cinnamon-flavored chocolate that the Spanish adore.
Their gaiety revived quickly and all the girls, nearly all
pretty and gracious, did their best to please us. This allowed
us to take several interesting pictures.

After a thousand thanks and a discreet tip to the
Master of the Chapel, we took the train next day for Cordova.

What a pretty town with its narrow streets, its grilled

windows, its patios ornamented with orange trees in flower.
In spite of oneself, one looked about for serenaders. But I
did not find the least vestige of the famous leather of Cordova.

Anatole did not share my enthusiasm at all. In the
evening, as we strolled along the Guadalquivir mirroring a
magnificent sunset, having in front of us the old Roman
bridge beside which rose the celebrated Mosque of the Hundred Columns, I said:

"Heavens, Anatole! Isn't it beautiful!"

He hardly raised his eyes from the cigarette he was
carefully rolling and, very calm, he said to me a bit disdain-
fully:

"As for me, what I see most clearly is that here I pay
three cents for my newspaper!"

I could have beaten him.

But I felt myself a bit at fault. Our trip to Cordova
had not been included in our voyage; it was for my personal
pleasure that I had added these hours to his exile. I understood his ill humor. He had difficulties with the cameras
whose adjustment was delicate and somewhat imperfect. Perhaps the Paris workshops were not entirely responsible for
that. He had to carry the camera most of the time. He was
tired of the rather monotonous cuisine...rice with chicken,
rice with fish, rice with shrimp. The hotels where we stopped
were not irreproachably clean. The streets, where women
combed or de-loused their magnificent hair before their
doors, where children slept almost naked on the sidewalk,
their eyes fringed with flies, smelled strongly of fruited oil.
And one grows quickly tired of dried peas and tourone.
That same evening we were going to Seville, hoping to find
the ideal Carmen. The cigarette-girls whom we met had,
without doubt, inherited the combative character of that
heroine, but unfortunately not her seductive charm. We had
to content ourselves with taking some documentaries: the
celebrated Giralda, the house of Adam, the sultan's garden
and his bath of which, despite my encouragements, Anatole
obstinately refused to taste the water.

And then there was Granada whose name evokes ripe
fruit, Granada whose light-colored houses scale the Albaicin,
whose narrow streets are silent at siesta time but on waking
echo with the noise of the hoofs of a hundred little donkeys
decorated with rainbow pompoms.

I shall not describe the Alhambra (Chateaubriand took
care of that) nor the magnificent gardens and water-mirrors
of the "Generalifa." Pictures, cinema, novels and perhaps
travel have familiarized you with the splendors of Andalusia.

It was in the Albaicin, thanks to a guide recommended
by our hotel, that we met the king of the Gipsies. Tall,
slender, no longer very young, but of a fine bearing, he was
certainly photogenic and his picturesque costume: high leg-
gins buttoned with gold, trousers, bolero and large Mexican
hat ornamented with multicolored braid and having pompoms
like those of the donkeys. The guide served as interpreter
and the king consented, for a fee, to present us to his people
and to organize some dances to the music of discs recorded
by the studios of Belleville.

He conducted us to the Calle de Jesùs where his tribe,
who seemed to have retained its complete autonomy, lived in
troglodyte quarters scooped from a landscape dotted with
cactus in a spur of the Sierra Nevada. Their perfect cleanliness surprised us. They had kept their customs, their
costumes, marrying within the group. Their costumes very
different from those of the Spaniards, were original and
strangely resembled those of Seminole Indians.

Almost all the young gipsies were handsome, with a
beauty at once hard and lascivious. The softness of their
brown eyes, veiled with long lashes was contradicted by the
cruelty of the smiles uncovering the teeth of carnivores.
Their dances, the immodesty of which would make an amateur
of modern dance smile, nevertheless made me fairly ill at ease.

The children, adorable babies, offered to dance for us,
for a few cents, the same dances as those of their parents.
I declined, but I had to accept the offer of a toothless old
sorceress who insisted on predicting my good fortune, while
pushing me towards a cactus full of threatening spines. I
put a piece of money in her claw, she muttered words which
I did not understand, but they must have been malevolent

for a setback with the discs and the motion picture camera made many of our films unusable. However, this was the high point of our journey and some of these dances were projected at the Hippodrome when that great theatre became the Gaumont Palace for the first demonstration of talking pictures.

We closed our voyage with a visit to Algeciras where the conference was taking place. It is not there that I would like to end my days. At the inn, the proprietor was quite astonished to see me refuse to inhabit the same room with Anatole. But, he insisted, "hay tres camas en el cuarto" ("three beds in this chamber"). I finally obtained a bedchamber with three beds, but alas, only one sheet, and Anatole went to bed elsewhere.

The next day we were served, on a wine-spotted tablecloth, "cafe con leche" and butter adorned with a fishbone.

We were happy to leave the country, however magnificent, and to refresh ourselves for a few hours at Gibraltar. We could admire, on the little beach, the Moroccan sheiks who had crossed the straits to carry to the unfaithful the fruits of their orchards, piled up at their feet in bright coloured pyramids.

We scaled the rock, teasing the little monkeys that inhabit it. We bought some filigree jewelry; lunched in a restaurant of meticulous cleanliness, and arrived at the barracks where two red-clad soldiers smilingly crossed their bayonets to forbid my entry.

Then we returned home, not without regret.

On arriving at the studios I made the acquaintance of Herbert Blaché, newly come from England where he assisted [A.C. and R.C.] Bromhead, the director of the London agency. He was taking a course of studies in the workshops and studios of Belleville, to familiarize himself with the technical aspects before returning to Berlin where he had just been named assistant manager.

I had planned with [Louis] Feuillade, aficionado [of bullfights] and well acquainted with the region, to go to film Mireille at Saintes-Maries-de-la-Mer. Anatole was tired and unwell; Gaumont decided that Herbert Blaché should take his

place, which would permit him to familarize himself with the
function of the motion-picture camera. He accepted without
enthusiasm. Later he told me that he had never met a woman
who was at first so cold, so distant as I. No doubt he was
right. Still young, in a job where I had to give proof of
authority, I avoided all familiarity. With my personal friends,
Feuillade among others, for whom I felt great sympathy, I
recovered my true personality. My youth and gaiety quickly
regained the upper hand.

It was at Nîmes that we made our debut. I had rented
from Olivier, then director of the arenas, the bull-ring for
the afternoon. The matador celebrated at the time was Machaquito, an idol whom I myself was desirous of knowing.

Olivier did me the honor to show me around the arenas.
I visited every room, including the chapel, the hospital and
the morgue, for bullfights sometimes end tragically. I made
the acquaintance of the picadors, and the unfortunate horses
whose last hour was approaching.

The stadium tiers were still empty, but one could hear
the humming, outside, of the impatient crowd.

In the door reserved for the personnel there was a
great arch flooded with light. Olivier signaled to me the arrival of Machaquito. He was a young man, not very tall,
thin, muscular, almost too graceful. His soft rose costume
entirely embroidered with gold glittered in the sunlight. He
approached us. Olivier made the introductions. Machaquito
bowed simply and went to his dressing room. The impression
was good. I rejoined my companions in a reserved loge to the
right of the loge belonging to the president of the arenas.

The doors were opened to the public: the bleachers
filled to overflowing. Little by little the noise and bustle
faded, and Machaquito at the head of the quadrilla and accompanied by the traditional music, entered the arena, welcomed by an indescribable ovation. He stopped before the
loge of the president, who threw him the key to the bull-
pen, then, turning toward our own loge he flung his hat,
thus dedicating the bullfight to us. The teasing of my com-
rades increased...how did they ever procure the bloody ban-
derillas with which they stuffed my valise?

I will not describe the bullfight, in which six bulls were killed. In spite of the cruelty of the spectacle, the courage of the matador stirred me often. The fight finished, Olivier was much amused by my emotion.

"Since Machaquito has made a conquest of you," he said, "I must go pay for his fight at his hotel. Will you accompany me?" I accepted.

Machaquito had retired to the patio of the hotel. Dressed in an old house-robe, in slippers, he smoked an enormous cigar (I've never seen the like of those in Spain). He received the silver, and our compliments stolidly and we parted certainly without regret.

The next day we left Nîmes to go to Saintes-Maries-de-la-Mer.

I did not know Provence. The Alyscamps, the necropolis at Arles, bordered with Franco-roman tombs and magnificent shade trees, was a revelation.

At Saintes-Marie-de-la-Mer, we were received by a group of mounted guardians, armed with their tridents. One of them dismounted and came to bow before me, his great hat sweeping the ground. My surprise at these lordly manners ceased when Feuillade introduced him: Marquis de Baroncelli-Javon, great friend of Mistral. He was a dedicated member of the Félibridge (the Society of poets and prose-writers formed in 1854 with the object of preserving the Provençal dialect), consecrating himself to the rearing of fighting bulls and the little white horses of the Camargue, who were born, he said "from the foam of the sea which deposited Aphrodite on the beach." The Marquise received us in the costume of Arles, in a farmhouse whose furnishings were entirely Provençal.

It was this nearly deserted Crau plain, overflown by rosy flamingos, where only a few mulberry trees set a little shade, but vibrant with perfume, with light, with its little tenth century church to whose pierced bell-tower Mireille came to die, that would serve us as stage. We revived the village corrida where the guardians rode, the pretty girls of Arles on the cruppers, where Mireille met her lover. The gathering of mulberries. The great bulls meekly letting

themselves be guided by the little white horses. The guardians so lively, so attentive, thank God, for without them the
enormous bull "Provence" (a killer with three dead men to
his record) would have gored us well and truly. Finally, the
crossing by the whole troupe of the little Rhone by moonlight
closed our excursion.

I felt a sadness in leaving this beautiful country. The
delightful evenings we spent under the tamarinds, listening
to Feuillade recite some verses of Mistral, watching for the
mirage which, almost every evening made a sunken city seem
to spring from the water.

We wanted to visit the arenas of Nîmes once more. The
setting was romantic. That evening made us regret our coming separation. I did not expect to see Herbert Blaché again.
On returning to Paris he immediately rejoined his post in
Germany. But we are only the toys of destiny.

Hardly a few weeks had passed when many of our German clients complained of the difficulties they had in assuring
the delicate interaction of the two elements of the chronophone
to obtain a perfect synchronization.

Gaumont, kept in Paris by important business, spoke of
delegating me to Berlin. I objected that I knew neither the
country nor the language. "That doesn't matter, you know
Blaché, don't you? He will accompany you and serve as interpreter."

Thus it was that in the company of Herbert Blaché I
discovered Germany. Berlin and its pretty environs: Unter-
den-linden frequented by German students with their military
bearing and scarred faces under little polo caps, tossing off
champagne in the company of big blonde girls who in no way
augured the slender and sportive German women of today.
Herbert Blaché showed me the castle of Sans-Souci where
Voltaire was humiliated and the miller repaid. It was with
Herbert Blaché that, while visiting our clients I discovered
Dresden, Nuremberg (that ravishing Renaissance city, cradle
of the Master singers, native town of Bach and Albrecht
Dürer. I never would have imagined, while I admired Nuremberg, that it would be the seat of the tribunal charged to
judge the worst war criminals), Frankfurt, Cologne, the banks
of the Rhine, etc.

Our clients proved amiable, their gallantry was a bit
heavy but they listened with attention and intelligence to the
explanations that Herbert translated for them.

I finished my task without too many difficulties. I had
made a fine journey. The romance, begun at Nîmes, arrived
at its conclusion. We decided that unless our sentiments
changed, we would announce our engagement at Christmas.

Some days before that holiday, Herbert Blaché arrived
in Paris, renewing his proposal and telling me that his father
would join us soon to make an official request for my hand.

But Léon Gaumont had another surprise for us. He
told us that he had ceded the exploitation of the chronophone
patents to two American entrepreneurs from Cleveland, Ohio,
and had promised to send them a specialist to aid them at the
start, and had chosen Herbert Blaché to occupy this post
because of his acquaintance with the language.

Two months later, three days married, I left my family
and my country with a heavy heart, persuaded that I was
abandoning my fine metier forever.

CHAPTER SIX

The crossing was gloomy. However, thanks to my brother-in-law who was attached to a travel agency, I had the most beautiful cabin on the bridge and my place at the captain's table. Alas, an ungovernable seasickness spoiled the voyage, which was lamentable both for my husband and myself. We arrived in New York at four o'clock in the morning. The view of Liberty lighting the world, the sight of the skyscrapers in the fog could not chase my sadness. I saw all that through tears which I tried in vain to stop. All around me I heard exclamations of enthusiasm in a language of which I understood not one word.

The customs agents, the police, the health service officers came out on the little tugboats charged with leading the big packet into its dock.

My husband had left to gather our baggage and to have our passports visa-ed.

The emigrants, grouped around their guide, women burdened with bundles, a swarm of children clinging to their skirts, the men with hands in pockets and cigarette butts at lip, anxiously waiting for someone to rule on their fate. Those whose papers were not in order or whose health seemed bad were sent to quarantine on Ellis Island where it would be decided whether to accept or to return them to their country. The luckiest were those whose family had preceded them, or those who were specialists in a trade whose skill was needed, these received their permission. They also received their first lesson in American courtesy toward women.

A big policeman, probably Irish (they all are) stopped one couple with a firm "Not here." He took the baggage from the arms of the woman and transferred it to those of the astonished husband, caressed the cheek of a sniveling brat, encouraged the mama with a friendly pat and a smile.

For us, the police and the customs personnel were amiable. We had filled out in satisfactory fashion the long questionnaire; affirmed that our jail record was virgin; that we were not bigamous; that we had the necessary fifty dollars; that we had been vaccinated, etc. Finally, we were young newlyweds and brought with us a considerable trousseau and furnishings. We would not be a charge upon the country. They even excused us from the customs duties.

A few moments later we came out on the Bowery, a shady neighborhood of New York frequented by all the undesirables. Amidst the animation of a great port, the workers invaded the old wagons transformed into snack-bars in the search for a hot dog and coffee. The elevated railroad still existed and made a noise like thunder. The tramways, of which some were still horse-drawn, crossed each other in every direction.

I wobbled, still feeling the boat's movement. At last an old coachman agreed to take us to the hotel Lafayette.

We could spend only a short time in New York. After a short rest, my husband proposed a promenade of discovery.

It was probably five o'clock when we arrived on Broadway. I thought there was a revolution. Every doorway vomited hundreds of human beings using their elbows and fists, shouting, swearing, calling each other. Jostled, dazed, I hung on the arm of my husband who seemed to find it all amusing.

"It's just the hour when work lets out and the employees hurry to rejoin their families, to find a little calm and fresh air in the Bronx, Manhattan, Brooklyn or elsewhere."

Tramways passed, with clusters of people hanging to their platforms. Interminable lines marked time impatiently waiting on the wharves for the ferryboats crossing the Hudson. Some were engulfed in the mouth of the subway.

"It'll calm down soon," said Herbert. And in fact, an hour later, the town was calm again.

We returned to the Lafayette, dead-tired, happy to find the American comfort and the excellent French cuisine to which we could at last do honor.

The hotelkeeper, to whom we recounted our first trip,
advised us to see the minuscule church and cemetery of the
first pioneers, to visit the Battery aquarium, one of the
world's richest (gone, today), to see the strange open-air
stock market where the brokers sat astride the window balu-
strades, calling their orders to employees waiting in the
street, noses in air, ready to rush off to transmit them. He
counselled us to see the Chinese quarter, the Bowery. All
that everyone knows today, thanks to the cinema and television, but which was for us truly the new world.

We soon had to leave all that to go to Cleveland where
we were awaited.

When we arrived at the depot, Grand Central Station in
New York, the melancholy that had lifted a little bit seized
me again. This was March. From the already black sky fell
an aggressive little hail that set itself to enter and scratch
the most tightly closed collar. In the long railroad car we
entered everything was somber; the stacked bunks were
closed with heavy leather curtains; the employee who relieved
me of my hat and put it in a sack, and slid our tickets in
the hatband of my husband, was black. He arranged our
little parcels in the numerous string bags hung around the
compartment, slid the valises under the bunks, indicated the
location of the toilets and the little lounge and left us for
newcomers.

The train started.

"You are tired," my husband told me, "go make your
toilette and go to bed. Things will be better tomorrow."

Meekly, I went off to the toilets, where I found twenty
or so women preparing for the night. The timidity and modesty of Latin people seemed out of place. In the wide-open
water-closet, a plump woman was in lively conversation with
a traveler busy putting her hair up in curlers. Seeing my
hesitation one of them took pity on me: "Here, dear, is a
free place. Oh! I see you are not Yankee...Frenchie I
guess?" Then each did me the honor of explaining for my
appreciation the American inventions, paper towels, mechanical dryer, protective seat-cover, etc. I smiled at all as well
as I could, but I was happy to get back to my husband who
waited patiently beside the little ladder which he had to climb
to mount into the upper berth.

I had trouble in sleeping. When I woke, we were arriving in Chicago. Boys came up into the car, offering coffee, chocolate, and buns for sale.

The porter sent us to wait a bit in the little lounge
car. A few instants later the beds had disappeared, replaced
by comfortable benches. Alas, the sky was black, the hail
continued to fall. The crossing of the prairies (so beautiful
under their wheat in the summertime) was gloomy. The train
announced with a bell its arrival in each village, which seemed
always the same. A big grocery, bars, a hotel where, on a
big glassed-in veranda, men rocked in rocking chairs, feet
in air or reposing on a bar of copper. A few farms and the
same landscape began again endlessly.

The natives of Chicago adore that city. I have visited
it several times. In spite of its lake and the beautiful build-
ings there reflected, it has always seemed hostile to me. The
industrial city, interesting in many ways, seems to me like
an enormous octopus whose long, far-stretching arms, slide
their suckers among the hovels of distant suburbs, forcing
into the gutter human beings whose resistance has been van-
quished by hunger. The scandals of the slaughterhouses
live in the memory of every reader of livres noirs.

Finally we arrived in Cleveland, of which we had been
told great things. An eighty-kilometer lake was the principal
attraction.... Alas, no lake visible. The train stopped by
an enormous garbage heap.

The purchasers of the chronophone patent had come to
meet us at the station. They led us to a rather luxurious
hotel where they had reserved us a room for the night. This
was a new surprise. The bedroom and the bathroom appeared comfortable and clean but the bed was absent. I pointed
this out to my husband. The bell-boy, questioned, pressed
a button on the wall: a panel leaned outward, disclosing an
excellent double bed where I stretched out with pleasure.

The next day my husband conferred with the new bosses
and installed me on the platform of an autobus making a
tour of the city. I made the tour three times, a little upset
before I found again the point of departure where Herbert
was waiting to lead me to the boarding house where he had
rented a room.

It was a strange boarding house where the father was
a minister (one could be married in the living room) and the
mother the inn-keeper, the son a baseball player, the daughter a nurse. There was also a black cook who made a conquest of one of the guests, was married in the living-room
by the pastor, and admitted to our table some days after our
arrival. I would have preferred that she keep her place in
the kitchen for she made succulent pies.

I had many other surprises in Cleveland. We lived on
Euclid Avenue, a principal artery, with a succession of magnificent dwellings almost all belonging (save for a few exceptions like our boarding house) to the diplomatic world, past,
present, or to come. A member of a prominent American
family lived across the street. Every morning, accompanied
by his grandson, he examined his garden fence and his heir
earned a penny whenever he found a lath to be replaced.
Poor man; for all his fortune, he could eat only milk and
toast. He made many donations to the libraries of the whole
world, it seems; but every time, he raised by a penny the
price of a litre of gas.

Euclid Avenue was traveled by numerous little electric
cars resembling a big armchair, driven principally by women.
They could not go more that eighty kilometres. One would
then have to recharge the battery.

I am indebted for all this information to a very charming and eccentric old Norwegian lady, Miss Andrupt, member
of a family of explorers who inhabited our boarding house,
spoke quite a little French, and who undertook to be my
guide and to teach me English. It was she, no doubt, to
whom I owe the notice taken of me by the Alliance Française
which invited me very kindly to their meetings and which I
attended during the few months of my stay in Cleveland.

I made many good friends and I began to learn the
manners and customs of my new country. For example, I
learned that I must not be stuffy if the daughter of our host
showed a lively taste for my husband, nor be surprised if
he, the day after our arrival, confided me to the son of the
family, who took me to watch a game of (I think) rugby. I
had the impression of living among madmen.

My wardrobe was a problem, I had such a pretty

trousseau, the work of my sisters and my mother, that all
the women wanted to examine it. But my dresses, made by
the stars of the great dressmaking houses, were all long and
American women had already adopted shorter skirts. The
first time that I wore the simplest of these dresses with a
train I was asked if I were going horseback riding. My hat
(from Reboux, if you please) was ravishing, but women here
wore hats rarely or never.

When Herbert took me to the theatre in one of these
dresses, it created quite a stir. John and Lionel Barrymore
were playing. I was ashamed and sorry that I could not
understand anything said by these excellent actors. Happily,
I learned quickly.

But time was passing. The patent-holders seemed to
make no great effort to launch the chronophone. They had
rented a hall in Detroit (which was not yet Ford-country)
and the lighting was bad, the projection execrable. No advertising had been made.

We had been more that nine months in Cleveland without receiving a penny in salary. We sent Gaumont an S.O.S.

Gaumont had just finished setting up a factory in Flushing, Long Island, for the development and printing of films
in the United States. He had had a little studio constructed
for the filming with chronophone. He recalled us to Long
Island then, and confided the direction of the group to my
husband.

In the United States the cinema was still in limbo, and
the Americans quibbled in attributing to Thomas Alva Edison
the invention of the cinematograph. Kinetoscope parlors
flourished in every country, it is true, but that does not in-
volve projection on apparatus such as one could see on the
boulevards of Paris.

Contrary to what has been said, the Lumière brothers
believed the exploitation of the cinema was worthwhile. In
almost the first days, they had signed a contract with M.A.
[Eugene?] Promio, permitting him to make a world tour, filming as many documentaries as possible, in order to satisfy
the increasing demands of their clients.

Promio himself recounts his voyage and the welcome he received in the United States, when he showed his first films, in L'Histoire du cinematographe by Michel Coissac.

I make no pretense to undertake the history of cinema in the United States. I confine myself to reporting what I have seen and heard.

The Gaumont studio was not being used every day. The temptation was too strong; I resolved to rent it and try making a few films.

I had engaged, as assistant, a former officer [Wilbert?] Melville, who, like many Americans, had done a little of everything. My command of English was imperfect and he was a valuable help.

Already an organization had been created [the Motion Picture Patents Company] which grouped the productions of the several existing companies, Essanay, Vitagraph, Biograph, etc. into a program to be distributed to the movie theatres, which were already numerous. To join this group, which was indispensable, one had to pay a rather large sum. We did so, and our company, Solax [founded on September 7, 1910], gained membership in this group.

We began with a series of cowboy films (the William S. Hart genre), with all that this means, such as you have seen a hundred times. These rough, honest, good people with their stubborn little horses more than once demolished my sets and put my poor talents as a horsewoman to a harsh trial, but I did like them. They even taught me how to swing a lasso. With them I did some good work and soon our company trademark was known and popular.

Then came military films. In Washington the 15th Artillery received us very well, with a fine lunch in their own mess, and a game of polo organized in our honor. Also, a cavalry charge which bore down on us, so that I thought my last hour had come. It didn't even brush me, but it left me with my legs trembling for some time. Thanks to this meeting we took some interesting films: reminiscences of the American war of independence and of the Civil War.

The Marines welcomed us equally well. The commander

of a dreadnought did me the honors of his battleship. With him I reviewed his men ranged on the bridge. Later they figured in a film and were as pleased as children.

Our company prospered, making appreciable profits, and as the Gaumont Studio proved inadequate we decided to build our own studio in Fort Lee, New Jersey, which was just then the center of the cinema.

As my husband was held by his contract with Gaumont, for a fairly long time I had to manage by myself, but I already had good co-workers. There was Melville whom I have already mentioned and Bauries, a Frenchman from Newfoundland, who was literally faithful until his death.

An electrical engineer, Max Mayer (whose name is unjustly forgotten for he was the voluntary victim of the first X-ray experiments) gave our studio an installation unique at that time: an entirely removable ceiling, real keyboard for lights, spot-lights, etc. Our cameras, projectors, printing, perforation, were by Bell & Howell, whose reputation is well known. Finally, our film supplier was Kodak, which had arrived at an unequalled degree of perfection.

We had no difficulty in finding builders or specialized electricians, the American studios being already, from that point of view, better equipped than our own. However, their ignorance of certain procedures really astonished me. The first time that I asked my cameraman to get a special effect (on that occasion, a man walking on the water) he told me that this was impossible. I had to insist and to guide him, step by step, to obtain a result which filled him with admiration and earned me his respect.

One film where I had used a system of masks that permit printing two different views of the same image, and obtain double exposure effects, so intrigued the cameramen that they begged me to explain by what means I had achieved that result.

The care brought to choosing the most favorable angle in photographing a fine landscape, or obtaining a beautiful light effect, by contre-jour, was noticed and brought me critical praise.

The Americans caught up quickly, thanks to their scorn for routine, their love of risk, their ready money and many other qualities. They learned quickly, and the First World War, paralyzing European industry, permitted them an advantage they have kept ever since.

The patents of Lumière, Demeny, Gaumont and others were defended, luckily, by good lawyers. Some companies, like Lubin of Philadelphia, were not ashamed to make negative counterparts of our films, with very bad results, anyhow. I met Lubin and asked if he continued this little trade. "It's not worth the trouble," he said simply.

However, America at the time recognized its debt to Europe. Rather frequently there were given, in the big cities, expositions called "pageants" in which pretty women (legion in the United States) artistically presented foreign products: beautiful Genoese velvet, jewels, pictures, silver, etc.

An important group of new companies was formed, some in New York, some in New Jersey. Stage actors more and more willingly accepted roles in the new art. Clubs were formed, fairs were organized, among others, there was a great annual ball given at the Waldorf Astoria.

This was the epoch of the melodrama. Films had now attained the length of 3,000 feet. In each of the reels, the public demanded a "punch" or suspense (remember Pearl White).

The Shadow of the Moulin Rouge, A Terrible Night, The Rogues of Paris [all released in 1913], and many others were all of this genre. The abduction of rich heiresses (always young and pretty), pursuit by a lover or detective, entrapment in boats, flooded dungeons, quicksands, etc. Anything went, if only there was a happy ending.

Art and reality were both lost there, surely, and the critics were not always very tender. Alas! "Advisers are not payers." Also, my best critics were the audiences with whom I mingled incognito. There I heard an impartial judgment, sometimes deceiving also, for the same film, coldly received on 45th Street might arouse enthusiasm on 125th, and vice versa.

This genre of film put me in touch with the daredevils who made a specialty of doubling for the stars in perilous moments. Some of them, themselves, proposed to us that they should leap from a bridge onto a moving express train, to be tied between the rails, or face wild beasts, or pass through a fire, etc.

The men did not always have the monopoly on courage. One of them, having offered to make a jump of twenty metres of horseback over a frozen river, bearing a woman on the saddle behind him, at the critical moment asked for a bucket of whiskey to stimulate the horse who refused to jump. He drank the whiskey and it was the woman who courageously gave the decisive spur to the horse.

Generally journalists attended our filming. It was not the least of my surprises to see how much interest in my modest self was shown by the press and the public. I rarely passed a week without being interviewed. If it was impossible for me to receive the reporter he would write his article anyhow, and thus I learned some absolutely unsuspected details about my beginnings, my family, my ancestors.

After submitting, in France, to concealment "under a bushel," in the "heroic" period, I had the right to be surprised. It is true that I passed for a phenomenon, as for seventeen years I had been the only woman film director in the entire world.

Sometimes the studio resembled a menagerie, as wild animals furnished us with excellent material. The trainer [Paul] Bourgeois brought me, one day, a magnificent tigress weighing six hundred pounds. He assured me she was gentleness itself and begged me to caress her through the bars of her cage, to encourage the actors. I admit that I felt a certain hesitancy, but a director must not be a wet hen; I did the thing, and Princess received my advances very nicely, purring under the caress and rubbing against the bars like a great cat. Vinnie Burns, an eighteen-year-old actress whom I had coached was the first to enter the cage.

But Princess caused me a terrible fright one day. Not far from our studio was an old stone quarry. We decided to do an outdoor scene there with Princess. Fortunately I had placed men armed with pitchforks on top of the wall, even

though Bourgeois promised me that the animal would not escape. Hardly was the cage opened when Princess cleared
the wall in a few bounds and made for the woods. The
grilled windows of a convent (in which my daughter was a
student) rose hardly five hundred yards away. I imagined
the terror of the children seeing that big wild beast. The
fright alone could harm a heart patient. I seized a pike myself, and at last Princess returned toward her starting point
and we locked her up again, with relief.

In spite of that experience, we drove her one day, in
an auto, up to the Bronx Zoo in New York, where the keep-
ers assured me that her condition was not rare, that Princess
was...abnormal. She was killed a few months later by a
tiger whose favors she refused. Lions and panthers proved
less gentle than Princess and gave us several scares.

In a scene representing the Hindu temple of serpents,
I was obliged to set an example again and, despite my re-
vulsion, to roll a serpent about my neck. The snake was
perfectly inoffensive, but the actor who played the High
Priest would perform only on the condition of my going first.
Two days later, the whole studio would do the same.

The Pit and the Pendulum [1913] of Edgar Allan Poe
was a hard trial for Darwin Karr, my young leading man.
We had imagined as a way to deliver him by cutting his
ropes...while he lies tied to the torture rack, waiting for
the fatal sweep of the knife...to confide this mission to gutter rats. The cords were copiously smeared with food to
attract the rats. They fulfilled their role marvelously, but
a few preferred fresh meat, came sniffing at the nose of the
actor and even penetrated the legs of his trousers. When at
last the ropes broke he was not slow to jump to his feet,
swearing there would be no retake.

We had the greatest difficulty in keeping the rats from
invading the studio. We had surrounded the stage with metal
plates, on which they would slide and be unable to get away.
They had to be destroyed on the spot. First we tossed into
their midst an enormous cat who, horrified, jumped the bar-
rier at one bound. Then it was the turn of my little bull-
dog, an excellent ratter...the unhappy beast was immobilized
at once by twenty or so rats who attacked him from every
vantage point. We had to rescue him from his miserable

situation. Finally, all the personnel took arms, cudgels,
clubs, and finally, not without difficulty, we won out. We
were happy to be rid of the rats, but forced to admire their
courage.

The film had an enormous success. I went incognito
to the first showing and had great pleasure in observing the
shivers and anguished sighs of the public.

Contrary to general opinion, filming often offers real
dangers. Mortal accidents are not rare. Fortunately we
never had anything of the sort to deplore, as we judged that
the best of films was not worth a man's life.

My husband often preferred to take a personal risk.
For my film Dick Whittington and His Cat [1913], in order to
illustrate the sinking of a pirate ship, we had transformed a
big old unused sailboat into a magnificent caravelle. The
gunpowder and the fuse to provoke the explosion being ready,
my husband, arguing that women lacked the sangfroid for
this, insisted on executing the task himself. But when the
wind had three times extinguished the fuse, he lost patience
and tossed the match directly into the powder. The blast
was thunderous. I was on the opposite bank with the cameramen and some journalists amused by my anxiety. I saw my
husband regain the bank in the little boat into which he had
fallen back, fortunately. Worried, in spite of that, I begged
my assistant to go get news of my husband. He had taken
refuge in a bar, where he lost consciousness. Seriously
burned on face and hands. It took weeks for him to mend.

The film offered many new effects that were successful.

Do not think that we neglected the artistic side of cinema. The United States offered sites of incomparable beauty,
imposing waterfalls, forests of giant trees, magnificent flora
and fauna.

We took the greatest possible advantage of that: the
most favorable hour for the best light, the setting sun
lengthening the shadows, a reflection in a rippling pond, the
wind making waves in a field of wheat; all that was studied
and used. One begins to recognize that the talking-pictures,
in arresting the very promising, very encouraging development of the silent cinema, have deprived it of a great deal
of poetry.

As Gilbert Cohen-Seat says in Essai sur les principes
d'une philosophie du cinema [1946]: "Nature has more place
in that than man. In the theatre drama limits itself to the
human world. With cinema, it is all life that lends itself to
the spectacle, communicating a total resonance to the soul."
But today's talking-pictures, you know, are filmed theatre.

Here is an anecdote that illustrates very well the interest taken by the American public in a woman's career and
the difficulty there is in pleasing "all the world and one's
father."

My husband and I often spent our evenings preparing
the scenarios that we would direct, in turn. We complemented
each other very well. Perhaps I was the more imaginative,
but he had a more critical, more realistic spirit.

We had taken as theme for one of our films the possibilities for understanding and happiness of a couple having
the same career, a subject that we knew well.

"The theme is good," Herbert told me "but treated too
seriously. We're not merely addressing ourselves to an audience of intellectuals, but one of peasants, also, of miners
and cowboys. One must lighten this with a few gay scenes."
From the commercial point of view, this observation was just.

At that epoch, the public was very interested in the
question of child labor in the factories. Children went to
work at eight or ten years of age. This was the subject
that I chose.

Goldilocks, little daughter of the couple, made friends
through the garden gate with a little black child, to whom
she told her secrets. This child swore deep affection and he
promised to help her escape. He tried his best and there
was a whole series of elopement, of nights passed in houses
under construction, of pilfering from bakery shelves, finally
engagement in a factory, where the parents and the police,
after days of anguish, found them.

On this occasion the professors at Columbia University
paid me the great honor of an invitation to give a talk about
the cinema to their students.

I objected, my English was faulty, I was no lecturer.
But my husband, being English, spoke the language perfectly, he understood the business as well as I did and it
would please him to satisfy the request.

"No, I beg you, it's you we want!"

"But why?"

"Because you're a woman."

I ended by agreeing, with what apprehension you can
imagine.

Upon my arrival, I found groups of men and women
students in the classroom, some seated on the ground. A
little platform had been prepared for me. I climbed up and
took some few seconds to find my voice. Finally, I gathered
my courage and chose a sympathetic face to address. I told
that one listener, as best I could, of the difficult beginnings,
our joy at each discovery, the hope we founded on the next
generation, and what they might draw from our discoveries.
I invited them to visit the studio. In short, everything went
as well as might be. I was asked to name a date for another
chat, but this time illustrated by the projection of one of my
films, and this second lecture would take place in the big
conference hall which held 3000 persons. Happily for me, on
that occasion the weather was dreadful and the audience was
small.

I chose to illustrate that lecture by the film which I
have just described. The conference over, I was surrounded
and complimented very politely, but many professors asked
me why, when treating so interesting a subject, I had thought
it necessary to weaken the theme by the trite little children
as intermediaries. There you are!

I remained on good terms with the Columbia professors,
and the pentagonal figure (of the university?) gave me the
idea of a little cinematography college which might take that
form, each branch being reserved for a particular science.
The idea seemed to interest them and if my stay in the United
States had been longer we would certainly have tried to do
something of the sort, Columbia University being disposed, it
seems, to finance the costs. Unfortunately, as with so many
other projects, this one died in the egg.

The trade of cinematographer was not always a happy
one. Concern for the truth obliges one to see and document
sources which are sometimes tragic. Thus, to set the stage
for an opium parlor, I visited the Chinese section of New
York accompanied by two detectives, the public not being
everywhere admitted. I assure you that was not gay. In
the stacked bunks the poor ashen-faced people, men and
women, anxiously awaited their pipes which a Chinese boy
prepared for them.

I have visited Chinatown since, being more familiar with
American life and having understood that I could risk myself
there without much danger. In the United States the Chinese
were still preferred to the Japanese. Numbers of them are
handsome, tall, very courteous. Their shops overflow with
beautiful things: their porcelain is famous, their cloisonné
vases, jade, fans and kimonos and thousands of other precious
things excited the desires of visitors.

The Chinese are particularly grateful. I attended a
reception that they gave to a teacher who had devoted herself to teaching English and familiarizing the children to life
in America. The hosts had thought of a thousand charming
little touches and chosen the dishes which might most please
her.

Their theatre alone deserves a detailed description.
Foreigners were accepted, but placed in a little section completely separated from the larger public. There were no
roles for women, or rather, the feminine roles were filled by
men in women's costume, imitating the high voices of women.
No stage decor. If the act was played in a forest, someone
carried on for the scene a few branches planted in a barrel.
The audience seemed either madly amused or terribly sadden-
ed. I have seen a Chinese theatre since, in San Francisco.
It had been Americanized and had lost much of its interest

Each month, foundling children were gathered together to be presented to married couples wishing to adopt a child or two. The State examined every case with care, to be sure of the moral quality of the candidate parents, of their resources, of their health. For the rest, the foundling pupils would stay under the surveillance of the Service until the age of eighteen or twenty years. For this occasion, the children were combed and dressed-up. Some were joyful; the older ones, those who had never found an adoptive family, were more fearful and anxious.

I visited this nursery with Olga Petrova, one of my most beautiful actresses, who pretended not to be able to endure children. All this little group, wanting so much to be adopted and to escape from that place, ran and hung upon her, examining her furs, her jewels, stroking her hands. Suddenly she disappeared. Upon leaving the asylum, I looked for Petrova and found her in a corridor, sobbing. We parted without a word.

Next there was the hospital for the incurable. There also American society did its best to lighten their suffering. Games, books, the phonographs of the period where at the disposition of the children capable of playing with them. Numerous nurses passed to and fro noiselessly, always ready to console, to comfort. These were mostly children afflicted with poliomyelitis. The nurses, with exemplary devotion, spent hours in helping them exercise, which it was hoped might return suppleness to the poor atrophied limbs. None of these children seemed truly unhappy.

On an island in the East River of New York, I visited a madhouse. We crossed the path of women walking together, a sad sight and not edifying. One of the guardian nurses insisted on having me meet her favorite. Isolated, ceaselessly weeping, her beautiful hair loose on her shoulders, she embroidered pretty tea-cloths. I bought a few, wishing with all my heart that she might be cured. Visit to the men's ward was short. On seeing me, one of them escaped his guards and flung himself at my feet, taking me for the Virgin Mary. Flattered but fairly frightened, I was delivered roughly by two guards who took the poor devil off. They assured me there were no padded cells in that establishment. Perhaps that old asylum has been demolished long ago.

I attended a Night Court session and came out of it in tears. They were judging a girl of fourteen caught soliciting in the street. She answered the Judge's questions in a weary voice.

"You have no family?"

"No, Sir."

"No friends?"

"No, Sir."

"I am obliged to send you to a reformatory. You are sick and dangerous. Try to get hold of yourself and mend your ways. We will help you."

"Thank you, Sir."

A jailer came to take her; she followed quietly. Someone beside me murmured "What about the men?"

In another case a young woman cradled a baby in her arms. She was afflicted with an acute case of venereal disease. She was condemned to six months of detention, but when her baby was taken from her arms she cried out piercingly "Leave me my baby, I beg you. Leave me my baby."

I had occasion to accompany out of the Tombs a poor idiot who one Sunday...an aggravating circumstance...had tried to kiss a woman against her will. He was put through all the anthropometric examinations, and then incarcerated in Sing Sing, sinister prison with sweating walls.

There I met in a corridor fifty or so prisoners on their

way to the dining hall under the escort of armed guards.
Heads shaven, dressed in the striped suit of the inmate, they
carried their food bowls under their arms. They stared at me
coldly. I was taken next to see the cells of those condemned
to death. There were fifteen there, locked into narrow,
barred cells, in the dark. Finally, I saw the famous electric
chair. The director was so kind as to invite me to sit in it.
I did so. They put the manacles on me and the director said
"Now, there is nothing to do but make contact...." I asked
if death were instantaneous. "Around eleven seconds," he
answered "some resist longer." He even invited me to attend
an execution which would take place the next day. I refused.
I have kept a photograph which I never see without a shud-
der.

My husband, having finished his contract with Gaumont,
Had taken the presidency of Solax. I abandoned the reins
to him with pleasure. I never attended any of the conferences
where the Sales Co. composed the programs; I would have
embarrassed the men, said Herbert, who wanted to smoke
their cigars and to spit at their ease while discussing business.

Herbert Blaché had directed, in the little Gaumont
studio at Fort Lee, a singer named Lois Weber who recorded
several songs for the chronophone. She had watched me direct the first little films and doubtless thought it was not
difficult. She got a directing job and certain Americans pretend that she was the first woman director.* My first film,
of which I speak in the first part of these memoirs, dated
from 1896.

In winter the Bay of Flushing resembles a polar landscape. An imposter whose name I forget [Frederick Albert
Cook?], pretending to have discovered the North Pole, asked
permission to reconstruct his cabin, lead his train and his
dogs out there, and to film his adventure. Thus it was done
and all America swallowed it. Then [Robert E.] Peary arrived
in his turn, and took the crown.

Two all-male social circles existed in New York. Once

---

*Lois Weber was the first woman director of American nation-
ality.

a year, once only, they admitted women. These were the
Elks, as I recall, who invited me.

There was always a special attraction. This time the
attraction was a dark young man, a pronounced Latin type,
well-bred, extremely shy: Charlie Chaplin whose fame still
lasts. Of course, I had already seen him in comedies by
Keystone and Mack Sennett, in which the principal roles con-
sisted of receiving or of throwing custard pies, and I admit
that I had not been particularly charmed. I learned to know
him better, later, in my last work period in California. I
went to see him in order to propose making Le Chapeau de
paille d'Italie [The Italian Straw Hat] which I had Americanized as well as I could. He was working with Jackie Coogan
on his film The Kid [1920].

"No," he told me "I intend to make films of more feeling. Besides, I never work on a scenario. I take no matter
what object and I ask myself what I can invent around that."

His office was somber, the walls painted in a color like
dried blood. He called my attention to them with a sweeping
gesture. "Here you see," he said, with a lightly bitter smile,
"the retreat of a comedian."

Little by little the halls of the suburbs were abandoned
and magnificent movie houses were opened. [William] Fox
had a theatre on Broadway. He invited me to attend the
projection of one of my films. There I had, for the first
time, the surprise of being presented to the public. The
lights of the hall were lowered, those of the projector flooded
my loge. The loudspeaker introduced me as the author of
the film which had just been shown. I had to rise, to say
some words of thanks. It was my first direct contact with
the public.

In 1912 Sarah Bernhardt already in ill health, a leg
amputated I believe, came to New York and Played Madame
X, as I recall, with a young leading man who resembled John
Barrymore a bit, but who was an execrable actor [Lou Tel-
legen?]. Réjane also braved the American public in Madame
Sans Gêne. I think it was [Adolph] Zukor, a Hungarian
immigrant, who first had the idea of exploiting successful
plays with stars of the first magnitude.

In 1913 Italy began to delight the public with naturalistic decors. Everyone still remembers Quo Vadis. I think it was at this moment that [D.W.] Griffith abandoned Biograph.

I have mentioned the annual ball given at the Waldorf Astoria Hotel in New York. On the bank of loges overhanging the great ballroom, each loge bore the name of one of the film companies: Vitagraph, Biograph, Essanay, Fox, Solax, etc. The directing personnel were installed there. The great doors at the back of the ballroom opened and, four by four, under lighting designed to enhance their splendid toilettes, the stars, starlets, heroes and heroines of the period slowly advanced, paused to salute the loges, paired off in couples, and the ball began. In the corridors, behind the loges, tables were installed and loaded with glasses of champagne and cookies for the use of the dancers.

It was on this occasion that I made the acquaintance of an excellent actor, John Bunny, who had already won notice in a Dickens tale from The Pickwick Papers [1913]. He suffered from a strange illness which, I think, aided him somewhat in comic roles. He was covered with enormous warts. We had drunk quite a bit of champagne. I wanted to revive myself a bit and went down into the ballroom. There I was drawn by the laughter I heard from one little group. I approached them and was taken into the circle which surrounded Bunny. Poor Bunny was resisting with all his strength the efforts of some excited young women to undress him, in order to see if the warts decorated the other parts of his body. I don't know if Bunny was able to hold them off. A friend seeing my embarrassment came to help me out of the crowd.

Naturally I read some French newspapers. One felt a growing disquiet, a threat of war. But I was far from sensing it so near. War seemed to me impossible, remote. However, the scorn, the insolence of some Prussians in my company should have opened my eyes.

When we heard of the assassination of the Archduke Francis-Ferdinand by a Serbian, and the results that that might have, we were stunned. Poor Belgium was neutral. The Germans invaded it nevertheless, then the north of France and Poland. I am, I admit, terribly chauvinist. Every painful report put me in a state of nervous distress.

I nearly had a fight, in front of the Times building in
New York, with a Prussian who shouted "The French are
absinthe drinkers and chasers of women, they must be brushed
from the earth." I was about to fling myself upon him,
but my husband restrained me. "You're not going to fight
with that madman?" I didn't need to. A group of Americans
arrived and fell upon the orator, giving him his punishment,
and my husband pushed me into our car.

My two children [Simone born 1908 and Reginald born
1912] had just had a bad case of measles. Herbert led us to
Weaverville, North Carolina, to wait for the end of the war.
This was a bittersweet period.

At once, a Franco-American committee came to see me
and invited me to join in their activities. I accepted whole-
heartedly. This meant rolling bandages for the Red Cross
hospitals; manufacturing candles to light the trenches with
rolls of paper soaked in fat; among other things. Traveling
lecturers came by to encourage the work. One of them, seeing me in the front row and recognizing my nationality, took
my son in his arms and showed him to the audience, saying
"It's for kids like this that we fight." Then he asked for
contributions and there were some big bills offered. I can
still see an old farmer (a real, bearded Yankee) saying, "I
have not much, but take my potato harvest, sell it and send
the money there."

I didn't want my children's education interrupted. Someone told me of a very kind teacher, the widow of a minister.
To carry the Gospel, her family had traveled on foot from
California, a donkey carrying their baggage and the little
girl. The pastor had recently died.

She grew very attached to my children. It was she
who led us on an excursion to a farm called "Strawberry
Farm" at the foot of a mountain, a farm so lonely, so back-
ward that the farmers still poured their own candles. They
lodged us in an old, half-ruined cottage, warning us "Don't
go looking for wood in the woodpile. We found six rattle-
snakes there yesterday." They threw an old mattress and
some coverlets on the porch. "Don't be afraid," said the
farm-wife "they can't climb steps." All that seems like a
fairytale, but I guarantee it's exact.

These good people had found a fine, well-dressed baby on their doorstep one morning. They adopted it, reared it, and made a fine cowboy of him. They gave him to us as a guide on the fairly rough climb up the mountain, my two children on the horse which he led by the bridle.

All along the climb our guide pointed out for us the little rivulets of limpid water. He led us across a ruby mine, whose director gave us a sample, a round stone which he broke in front of my astonished children, and which looked inside like a pomegranate full of red crystals. These rubies are reduced to powder for emery-paper, only the most beautiful being reserved for jewelry. Finally we reached the hill's summit. Our cowboy took us to a cool spring hidden under rhododendron and mountain laurel of all colors. Truly, an Eden.

My son was four years old. He asked, suddenly "Mamy, the cowboy...couldn't we take him to New York to be my nurse?" This embarrassed our guide very much, but he, also, was attached to the child and they exchanged a friendly kiss in parting.

I could write many pages on our Carolina journey. There was, at Hot Springs, a camp for German prisoners. They were in fresh air, well treated, fat and arrogant as ever.

But we could not halt our activities much longer. My husband called me back and I returned to the studio. The return was not without its adventures. Our train was transporting American troops to embarkation from New York. Fifty kilometers out of Washington a freight train coming from the other direction was derailed and its last cars were thrown across the rails of the express. This was about ten or eleven o'clock in the evening. I felt a violent shock and then all the valises fell on my bed. My children woke up terrified. I dressed hastily in a peignor and went out on the platform.

"What happened?" I asked an employee running by with a lantern.

"Nothing, ma'am. Go back to your car."

"Oh! Excuse me but something did happen and I want to know what!"

I jumped on the track-bed and almost at once I saw the overturned locomotive across the route, its unfortunate driver and his aide crushed under the weight. Help came quickly but the poor men were dead.

We stayed there ten hours on the track. The soldiers were very attentive to me and did their best to help me. Finally, a rescue train came out to pick us up and returned us to Washington.

After a few hours of rest, we took a train again and arrived at last in New York, then in Fort Lee, New Jersey, where I immediately took up my activities again.

CHAPTER EIGHT

The Lumière and Gaumont patents having come into public domain, the industry was transformed. The Sales Company grouped its members to form a trust [Motion Picture Patent Company], in spite of the law.

Our company was sufficiently important for the new group to offer to buy it for a good price: two hundred thousand dollars, payable in shares (payables en actions) and to contract us for five years to one of their companies with a salary of six hundred thousand dollars for us as a couple. We decided against this offer, unpleasantly impressed by their methods (they threw the account books out the window and ...their guns spoke). However, a year later their business had quintupled. One had to accept appearing on their programs, or disappear.

Solax was transformed again and became, for over eighteen months under the name of Popular Plays and Players, the supplier for Universal, World, Metro, Pathé and others. We were rightly called "suckers," fish who take not only the bait but the hook.

My husband had allied us, without contract, to a stage director, [Lawence] Weber whose role was merely to furnish us stars, and books, popular plays which one had to pay dearly to adapt to the cinema. An anecdote will make clear what effort was needed to get this agreement fulfilled.

I had just finished directing The Tigress [1914]. All my "stock," that is, the actors regularly attached to our company were idle.

I forgot to say that M.H. [Aaron Hoffman?] had reserved to himself the right to sign the scenarios which I had written and that he told me candidly: "Don't break your head over it. I've given them the same thing for the last ten years and they never know the difference."

To return to my subject, I was given as a scenario
exactly ten lines of a poem by R.W. Service, "My Madonna"
from which I was to create three thousand feet of film. I
lost patience and grew angry.

"Come on, Madame Blaché," Weber told me "you'll manage very well. There's a free office here; I'll give you a
secretary and between now and tomorrow you'll have written
your masterpiece...."

I had no choice. The stock and the studio were immobilized (a great loss) while I took my medicine. I resigned
myself and I was imprisoned, literally. I must say that I
did not lack for beer and sandwiches and the secretary was
diligent. At midnight, I had finished the scenario.

I will not swear on my honor that the situation was
entirely new, nor that I never plagiarized. Mr. H was not
wholly wrong. The scenario was judged to be excellent, the
press was unanimously flattering and Olga Petrova received
quantities of letters of this sort "Olga Petrova, my Madonna,
life is richer thanks to you. All should pay you royal hom-
age, my Madonna, and they do."

Olga Petrova was already known and loved by the public, but she was difficult to direct. One day I wanted her
to play a scene of jealousy. "No," she told me "when the
hyacinth is faded it is I who will throw it away...."

However I made many films with her that had great
success:

The Tigress [1914], Scenario and direction by Alice
Guy Blaché.

The Heart of A Painted Woman [1915], adapted and
directed by Alice Guy Blaché.

The Vampire [1915], adapted and directed by Alice
Guy Blaché.

What Will People Say? [1915], adapted and directed
by Alice Guy Blaché.

Catherine Calvert [who starred in two 1917 features,

The House of Cards and Behind the Mask] was not one of the
artists whom Weber procured for us but had been sent to us
by the Seligmann bankers to whom, unfortunately, we had
been forced to have recourse. The Seligmanns had bought
half of our shares, plus one, and this gave them control.
She was their protegée and it was hard not to use her, although she limped badly. Here are two anecdotes that will
demonstrate how she showed me her gratitude.

The wife of a film director in the United States must
arm herself with a certain shield of indifferences. Many
actresses are willing to pay any price. I had then, as I
said above, engaged her myself in spite of her limp, this
pretty woman recommended by our creditors. These latter
asked us one day to take her with us to a reception in the
New York suburbs, given by [Lewis J.] Selznick to introduce
one of the Talmadge sisters whom he wanted to launch. En
route, Catherine Calvert suddenly said to my husband:

"You know, Mr. Blaché, for a director who would make
me a star there would be no limit to my gratitude."

"You might have to step over corpses," answered Herbert.

"Oh! That wouldn't bother me!"

One of my assistants warned me that she had broken
more than one marriage.

On arrival, we found a superb table set for the meal
at which Selznick would do the honors. He was not handsome, Selznick....

"Why don't you propose your trade to Selznick?" I
asked our companion.

"How horrible!" she cried, disgusted. Then added,
with half-closed eyes "But Mr. Blaché is so romantic!"

I had another little adventure with the same young
woman. We had gone, my husband and I, to do some Christmas shopping in town.

"Look, we are in the neighborhood where Miss Calvert

lives, and I have some details to give her on the film we're
starting tomorrow," Herbert told me. "I want to go see her.
That will advance us a bit."

"Excellent idea. I'll accompany you."

Herbert said nothing, but no doubt he thought a bit
about it anyhow.

In the private apartment-houses of New Jersey, one
must, before taking the elevator have oneself announced by
the doorman who telephones to inquire if the visitor may be
admitted. Preceding Herbert, I reached him first: "Please
announce Mr. Blaché," I said, slipping money into his hand.
He seemed to understand (Miss Calvert was not very amiable
with servants). He responded with a wink and did as I
asked.

When the elevator arrived at the floor indicated, the
door opened softly and Miss Calvert appeared in the most
charming and most revealing of dressing gowns. She had
pluck. Her smile of welcome was no less warm. She gave
both of us a very kind reception.

I had many troubles in the United States when I worked
for a French company [Pathé].

When M. [Marcus] Loew (I believe) decided to make
some superproductions and put me in touch with Bessie Love
and her mother, for the direction of the film The Great Adventure [1918], I suddenly sensed a reticence among the
personnel. I was called before the authors, or adaptors, of
the scenario.

"The scenario has been studied, Madame Blaché, you
have only to follow our indications."

"Very well."

"The action takes place in Florida. Some big Southern
citrus growers who want the publicity will make it possible
for you to visit the Everglades. We'll leave you the choice
of setting, etc."

So we started out with Bessie Love, her mother, Chester

Barnett, the leading man, his aunt Miss Flora Finch who was
a priceless English comedienne. Everything went perfectly.
Fine weather, magnificent landscape, Seminole Indians, crocodiles, floating forests on a great island of coral. I remembered the advice of the committee and tried not to get too far
from the beaten path. Returning, when we projected this
first part they reproached me for lack of imagination.

The voyage alone was worth all my troubles. Most
visitors stopped in Miami. If they went down as far as Key
West they would discover forests of dead trees, drowned in
the marshes, their branches overgrown with Spanish moss.
A narrow asphalt trail bordered them. A long strip of bark
seemingly fallen from the rotten trunks floats on the water.
Look carefully, you will see two eyes that follow you under
heavy eyelids, a maw armed with hooked fangs to hold its
prey, a terrible tail that could break your two legs with one
blow. Run! A little farther, night falls and great pimpled
frogs will jump on your lap. They are not dangerous, but
how nauseating. Before coming to the sea, you will pass
through cocoanut groves. I hope none fall on your head....

The beach is bordered by little dead trees and the
waves leave semicircles of minuscule dead fish in the sand.
The buzzards, voracious birds of prey, rush down on these.
This is the Bay of Mexico. Here in Florida were built all
the great hotels where the richest families of Washington,
New York, and other big towns pass the winter, and where
the pretty Yankee girls go water-skiing.

For my part, I was content to go see the bottom of the
Gulf. To do this, one had to hire a life-guard and rent one
of the light boats, a sort of raft composed of two oblong
floats united by wooden benches. Seated on one of the
benches, supplied with a bucket whose bottom was composed
of glass sheets, one must cross the breakers, to arrive in
calm waters and there let down the little bucket to view the
depths.

The Gulf contains the most beautiful submarine gardens
I have ever seen: corals, fish of all sizes and colors, sea-
stars, abalone, octopus. It took the sunset to draw me back
to the earth. I have seen the underwater gardens in Cata-
lina. They are only a pale copy.

On the beach, the black women, former slaves, cooked excellent meals. Broiled lobster, country-fried chicken, on which we feasted. There I tasted turtle eggs, a bit thick but not bad, and tiny corns on the cob, grilled in their leaves, which were called "gentleman farmers," and many other excellent things.

I have photos to illustrate the type of Indians we met. Their striped costumes, their lacustrine houses, the little crocodiles that we bought from them and who were part of the last nest we saw, containing thirty little crocodiles....

The citrus planters urged me to buy a farm which they offered to cultivate for me for three years. I have sometimes regretted refusing that offer.

For its part, the studio had kept some disappointments for me. In my absence, an excellent decorator who replaced Menessier for me had been dismissed as too expensive.

Finally Loew called me in one morning. When I arrived at his office he greeted me rather coldly: "Come," he said, preceding me toward the projection room. Already the projectionist was at his post. They rolled for me a frightful bit of film where pallid people moved against a livid sky.

"What do you think of that?" he asked me.

"Frightful," I answered.

"Well, why did you do it?"

"But that's not my film," I said, dumbfounded.

Doubtless Mr. Loew understood.

But that was not all. With a good deal of trouble I had arranged for the girls of the Ziegfeld Follies to play a scene, one Sunday morning, in which Bessie Love should appear among them. A date was set and directions given for the scene and the dressing rooms were ready on time. When I arrived at eight o'clock all was ready, but in the very center of the set, at an angle in view of the camera, a monumental column had arisen. We had to wait while the workers demolished this obstacle. I could hardly contain myself, I admit.

Some days later the studio director called me, "The administration finds that filming is becoming too costly. They want to give you one week's notice."

My husband himself directed a film for the same group. He had seen my efforts, and the first projections. He encouraged me as well as he could. I was not too sure of myself; comedy is much more difficult than drama. However, some weeks later the director of Pathé (whose name I forget) told me the film had been a success. Bessie and her mother were pleased and sent me a kind word about it, but the Pathé company abandoned the superproductions.

I also directed The Lure [1914], a celebrated play of the Shubert tour, with Julia Moore, for World. Concerning The Lure, I would like to recount some of the quarrels I had with the censors and with the distributors.

The distributing company reserved to itself the right to accept or reject productions...we had to take all the risks. Mr. [William] Brady, the representative of Shubert Features asked me if I would agree to adapt and direct The Lure, warning me that several directors had refused because they thought the subject too delicate. It concerned prostitution, the "White Slave" traffic. I had attended a performance. The play and the actors, Julia Moore among others, pleased me.

I had a certain acquaintance with the subject which was of public interest, as I had met a young lawyer who was especially concerned with it and who gave me some curious details about the activities of the gangster pimps. So, I accepted on condition that I might use the same actors who had played in the theatre production.

It was agreed that if the film was accepted, all the costs of production would be divided, as well as the profits.

Once finished, the film had to be submitted to the censors. The committee, composed that day of two old maids and a priest, refused it. I appealed, objecting that a decision was valid only if taken by a committee of at least nine people. New convocation. This time the committee was more than full: twenty or twenty-five persons. The chairman asked me to defend my film. I responded that I was completely

ignorant of the jury's objections. The chairman then asked
for a spokesperson from the jury. A young woman rose:
"The subject is scabrous," she said, "and I think that only
a woman could treat it with this delicacy. I think that Madame Blaché has succeeded very well." So the film passed unanimously.

I was not at the end of my troubles. Now I had to
get the acceptance by the distributing firm. I went then,
to submit my film to M.B.. During the projection, which is
usually sacrosanct, the director was called twenty times to
the telephone. He excused himself and asked me to leave
the film with him to examine it at leisure. He would let me
know.

Next day he called my husband. "Madame Blaché,"
he said, "has not come up to her reputation this time. The
film is mediocre. Let's make a deal. I'll offer you reimburse-
ment of costs and ten thousand dollars (according to our
contract, the profits should have been divided equally).
Under these conditions we'll take the risk of launching it."
A husband easily doubts the talent of a wife. Mr. Blaché
accepted the trade. This news infuriated me. I knew in
what a wasp's nest he had fallen.

Two months later I met that person again.

"I have good news to tell you," he said.

"That would surprise me."

"Just think: The Lure is one of our best money-getters,
in two months it has brought us three-hundred thousand dollars in profits...."

In this trade one must know how to hold one's tongue.
But the lesson was not lost. For example, there was The
Empress [1917] with Holbrook Blinn and Doris Kenyon for
Pathé. The same company having engaged Holbrook Blinn
(himself director of the Princess Theater and a well-known
actor) could not, for various reasons, use him and asked me
if I would consent to take up his contract and the scenario
on my own account, under the usual conditions. Tempted
by the fame of the actor, I accepted.

Alice Guy at the time of her marriage.

Top: Alice Guy (center) with the stars of her first film, La Fée aux
  choux, Yvonne and Germaine Serand.
Bottom: Triste fin d'un vieux savant (1904).
Opposite: La vie du Christ (1905).

Simone, Herbert, and Alice Guy Blaché.

Top: Alice Guy Blaché with her first car at Flushing, Long Island, in 1908.
Bottom: Directing Gaumont Talking Pictures.

Top: The building of the Solax Studios at Fort Lee, New Jersey.
Bottom: Alice Guy Blaché enjoying her work at Fort Lee, New Jersey.

An advertisement for <u>Dick Whittington and His Cat</u> (1913).

Above: Claire Whitney, one of Alice Guy Blaché's favorite actresses.
Opposite: Simone Blaché with other young actors in <u>The Violin Maker</u>
<u>of Nuremberg</u> (1911).

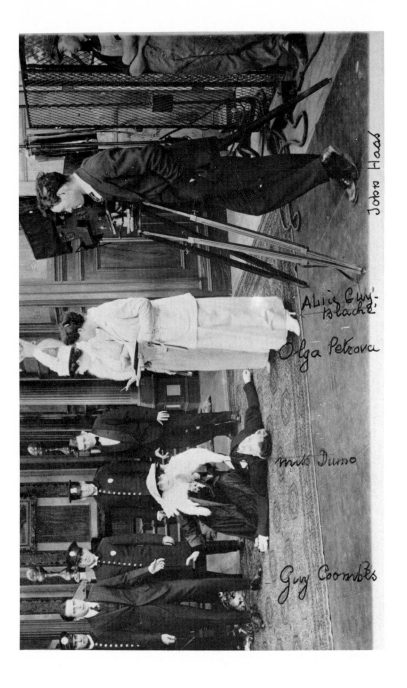

John Haas

Alice Guy-Blaché

Olga Petrova

miss Durno

Guy Coombs

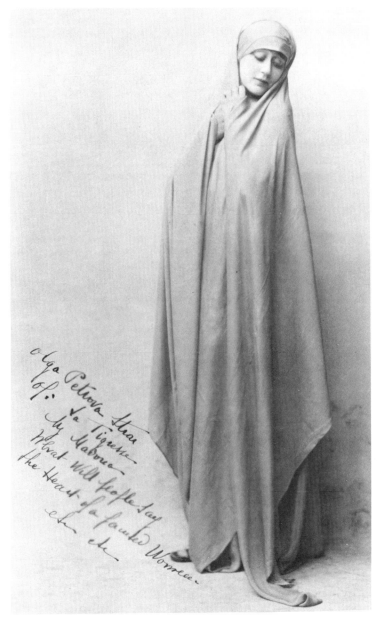

Above: The best known of Alice Guy Blaché's stars, Madame Olga
Petrova.
Opposite: Directing Madame Petrova and Guy Coombs in My Madonna
(1915).

Top: Flora Finch and Bessie Love in <u>The Great Adventure</u> (1918).
Bottom: On location for <u>The Great Adventure</u> (1918); Alice Guy
Blaché is under the umbrella and Bessie Love in the foreground.

Top: Bessie Love and Flora Finch in The Great Adventure (1918).
Bottom: Chester Barnett in The Great Adventure (1918).

Above: Herbert Blaché in the mid-twenties.
Opposite: Dolores Cassinelli in <u>Tarnished Reputations</u> (1920).

Gladys Moon Jones sculpts Alice Guy Blaché when she was living in Washington, D.C., in the fifties.

Holbrook Blinn proved perfect, as docile under direction as the simplest extra, and as I told him, recognizing his value I would willingly have accepted his suggestions. He answered me "The scenario is not very good. I am surprised that you're able to get so much out of it." He agreed to reread it with me. We made a few changes. He became an excellent friend.

At the presentation, the distributors tried to play the same trick on me as they had used with The Lure. I took my film away, without a work, and went directly to offer it to Pathé, who accepted on the spot at a better price than I had hoped. It was my turn to smile in reporting this good news to cynical Mr. B.

Many companies had emigrated to California, seduced by the climate and the beauty of the site.

The inhabitants were distrustful, one could often read over their doors the unflattering legend "No dogs or moviemakers."

A whole group of French directors worked for the World Film Corporation: Albert Capellani, Emile Chautard, Maurice Tourneur, etc. This company had not deserted Fort Lee. I had occasion to do some little service for Capellani and for Chautard and we became friends.

In my own studio I directed, for World, The Lure, which I have discussed already.

Griffith, Thomas Ince, and Mack Sennett joined to form the Triangle Film Corporation. Griffith had introduced Lillian Gish in the great film which made his reputation, The Birth of a Nation [1915]. His next film, Intolerance [1916], had a less enthusiastic press.

It would be useless to try and describe the state of the American cinema during the World War. There was a constant criss-cross of company mergers and annexation of newcomers if they showed merit.

A Hungarian immigrant, Adolph Zukor, was particularly active in the realignment of the market. He began as janitor in a fur-shop, of which he later became the proprietor.

Of uncommon intelligence, he quickly understood the impor-
tance of the cinema. He became treasurer for Marcus Loew
who managed both cinemas and vaudeville. He bought the
American rights for big foreign productions: the films of
Sarah Bernhardt, Réjane, Lucien Muratore and Lina Cavalieri.
He hired famous stage stars to make cinema.

Impossible to name all those whom fortune favored.

Between 1914 and 1917 there were few war films. The
Americans, as I said, were sympathetic but did not display
their feeling, except perhaps for Nazimova who, on the stage,
played War Brides [1916]. All that changed when America
decided to join the dance. The biggest stars made propaganda for military registration. Charlie Chaplin himself made
Shoulder Arms (Charlot Soldat). There was Harold Lloyd,
the smiling daredevil, competing with Douglas Fairbanks,
whose romance with Mary Pickford had begun to entertain the
studios. Francis X. Bushman, whose success I never could
understand, and who was, in my opinion, the worst of Romeos,
was at the height of his popularity. The Barrymores were
dazzling. Who has forgotten John Barrymore in Dr. Jekyll
and Mr. Hyde? The Madman? Don Juan? I have never forgotten Lionel Barrymore in Strange Interlude among others.

One of the Columbia University professors with whom
I had kept up friendly relations advised me to visit a sociology
professor, Mrs. Rose Pastor Stock of whom people told scan-
dalous tales. Why?

"Go see her, she's an advocate of birth control."

Madame Rose Pastor Stock lived in New England in a
tiny bungalow. Dressed in an overall and sandals, her hair
loose to the wind, she was working in her garden. "In fact,"
she told me "I encourage birth control. I have taken work
in a factory in order to mingle with women workers. I try
to gain their confidence. Have you seen some of the hovels
in Brooklyn where many families live in a single room? Where
the woman who is always pregnant may lose courage and ask
help of an abortionist, who may leave her mutilated for life,
if not dying? What I advocate is that a loving couple not
fear to unite, taking precautions, so that they may have
children when they desire them, and can care for them, and
rear them to be healthy. I have discussed this with priests
who have encouraged me."

Madame Pastor Stock was the wife of the proprietor of one of the great hotels in New York. She saw few people. She was always ready to help someone in misery. Living with her she had a blind black man whom she fed herself. It is said she gave asylum to Gorki. She was sentenced to ten years in prison, which she has not had to fulfill.

I suggested to Selznick that he make a propaganda film with her. He laughed in my face.

She gave me one of her published books, which I have lost in my travels. I regret it.

The Armistice, which I had so much wished for, arrived. I saw on Fifth Avenue in New York the enormous, joyful celebration, as only America can do them.

My husband, in middle-age crisis, had gone to California with his principal actress. I had to put my children in boarding school and rent a little apartment in Bretton Hall. I didn't know what I was going to do, when [Emile] Chautard advised Perret, who was busy with another production, to give me the direction of a film with Dolores Cassinelli which he was unable to make [Tarnished Reputations, 1920].

The salary was skimpy, two thousand dollars, six weeks of work, publicity at my own cost, but it was better than nothing and could put me back on my feet. I accepted.

The Cassinellis, mother and daughter, were charming. "If the film is good," they told me "we will put a big electric sign up on Broadway, with your name as director." I accepted.

"I'll give you the scenario bit by bit," [Leonce] Perret told me. "In the meantime, give them flowers and ribbons ...they like that...."

But the scenario was slow in coming. What's more, I had to wait until the studio personnel had finished with Perret before they paid any attention to my needs.

Osso, his publicity chief, more smart than honest, had me sign a contract for a hundred dollars a week for advertising I never saw.

One evening, irritated by my insistence, Perret told
me "O.K., I'm dining with Osso and his girl this evening,
you can come too. Afterwards we'll go and work at my
place."

That evening he took us to I forget what hotel. At
the table he sentimentalized, watching the couple. "Isn't it
beautiful, a happy woman?" Suddenly I saw him push his
plate aside in disgust. "How horrible," he whispered. I
gazed at him in surprise. "Didn't you see? She ate cheese
...cheese on those rosy lips...!"

The dinner ended and we finally started for the hotel
where Perret lived. We settled in the salon. Hardly had we
prepared tablets and pencils before Madame Perret joined us.
"I'm going to call a taxi for you," she said. "But Madame,
we're only beginning!" She hardly glanced at me. We heard
her use the telephone and soon a taxi arrived. And Perret,
theatrical, brushing his brow "You see my life, Madame
Blaché."

I finished the scenario somehow. The Cassinellis were
contented and the famous electric sign was ordered. But
Perret fretted "I can't tolerate that; I am the producer." I
was vexed myself: "It's the one profit I'm drawing from this
wretched affair, and I won't give it up."

However, it was this same Valentine Perret [Leonce's
wife] who devoted herself to my care. It was the time of
the Spanish influenza epidemic. The film had to be finished,
cut, titled; Perret telephoned that he was waiting for me at
his place. I felt very ill, feverish, and resisted. Valentine
came to the hotel in a car, to get me. "Come on, let's go,
don't play the wet hen. If you're sick we'll take care of
you." I had to obey. Hardly arrived, I lost consciousness.
The Perrets, anxious, called a doctor who came that evening.
His diagnosis was immediate: Spanish flu.

"She'll have to be taken to the hospital," said Perret
sharply.

"Impossible. There isn't a bed left."

"Very well. We'll care for her here," said Valentine.
Aided by the doctor they carried me to the attic. I was

settled in a bed with opaque curtains, and every day at the
scheduled times, Valentine, dressed like a nurse, came to
give me the necessary attentions.

That influenza was truly terrible. Five members of my
company were infected, four died. I don't know if Valentine
is still alive. I hope she has been rewarded. [She died in
1950.]

My husband, passing through New York, came to see
me. I believe my sad look moved him. He asked me to rejoin him as soon as I could. Six weeks later, with my children I took the road for California.

We made the New York-Chicago trip by night. When
we arrived in Chicago where we had to pass a few hours waiting to change trains, it was deep night and the glow of the
smelters made it look like a real inferno. The journey went
on, banal enough, with stops to take on water, through
prairies of sagebrush. A cowboy undertook to race the train.
Then we stopped on a Navajo Indian reservation. People
brought fragile pottery and copper necklaces for sale along-
side the train. "You have time to visit the village" said the
conductor.

In their huts the Indians beat the copper to make plates
and drinking vessels. The women card wool and weave handsome blankets and carpets, famous everywhere in the United
States. Women carry their babies on their hips; sometimes
they seat them on two branches attached at an angle, pulled
gently by a little horse.

The village of Albuquerque is frequented by many artists. The Navajo are proud, sad and handsome. Scattered
on the surrounding hills one can see a few isolated tents.

It was night when our train entered the great Colorado
desert. Another fairyland! We stayed until morning with
our brows pressed to the windows. There was sand, great
slabs of stone, giant cactus bearing flowers and fruits, enormous stars that seemed to hand within reach, and on the
corners of the blocks of stone, doubtless wet with dew, minuscule rainbows. The howl of coyotes was like an orchestra.

At last we came to the Rocky Mountains: enormous

peaks, fine trees, waterfalls, tunnels. No animals in sight...
frightened by the train, no doubt.

My husband met us in Los Angeles and led us to Hollywood. He had rented an apartment in a pleasant hotel on
Sunset Boulevard, at the foot of a hill planted all the way to
its summit with a Japanese garden. The hotel itself had a
fine garden of exotic trees where sometimes a flight of little
parrakeets would settle. There I saw and smelled a skunk
for the first time.

I found most of the actors there whom I had known.
Sunset Boulevard was very lively. Actors strolled casually,
still in costume, shopping for a meal, a drink, cigarettes.
Soon I also was recognized and welcomed.

Hollywood was not all beautiful gardens. Oil was still
important and the derricks rose everywhere. Hundreds of
workers were employed in drilling. Many houses were lighted
and heated by natural gas.

In the naphtha wells were found the heads of tigers
with elephant tusks. I have seen strange little red crabs
drawn out of the wells, perfect copies of a Japanese mask.
There was much to interest a scientist.

Hollywood smelled of eucalyptus or of petrol, according
to the direction of the wind. The studios were built as far
as possible from the derricks.

Hollywood Hotel was quite gay. There was a ball at
least once a week, often cut short by an act improvised by
one of the tenants: Jim Corbett ("Gentleman Jim") organizing
a fight with Milton Sills.

I was not particularly gay and I often took refuge in
the billiard room. My two children adored that and even my
baby, crawling on top of the pool-table, tried to manipulate
a billiard cue heavier than he was.

I wanted very much to go down to Mexico. But unfortunately, I was the victim of a hold-up, my car was terribly wrecked and my daughter hurt. The tragedy would
have been complete if a group of five automobiles had not
arrived at the spot and set the gangsters to flight. A doctor

was among the rescuers. He bandaged my daughter and we
continued on to the next town where she could be cared for.
I had to abandon my car to the insurance people and we took
the train back to Los Angeles. Two weeks later I went back
alone to retrieve my automobile and returned by the the
ledge-like road between the Pacific Ocean and the Sierra
Madre. It would need a long chapter to describe the beauties
of that route....

Herbert Blaché directed The Brat [1919] and Stronger
Than Death [1920] with Nazimova. I had become his assistant, rather, but with very long intermissions.

New religions were constantly coming to light: the-
osophy, new science, Christian science. I visited the cen-
ters, was taken by the abundant literature and was finally
invited by the Christian Scientists to visit and discuss the
scenario for a propaganda film. On the agreed-upon day, I
went to the rendezvous and was given a few pamphlets which
I read. I was shocked to see the way in which they treated
the Christian religion; its priests were charged with all the
sins of Israel.

I said "I understand that you value your faith, but is
it truly necessary to drag others in the mud in order to witness that faith?" There...the priestess cut me short.

"Ah!" said she "Are you Catholic? Useless to go any
further, you cannot work for us."

Tired of hotel life and for private reasons also I had
decided to rent a little bungalow. Nazimova, who had become
attached to my children, came often to visit us. She herself
had a very agreeable house on Sunset Boulevard where we
were often invited to tea. While my children played in the
garden she questioned me about French literature and music.
I did my best to inform, happy that someone loved my country. For her I hummed the "Chansons Tristes" of Duparc,
which she adored.

During one of these visits we learned that the Prohibi-
tion Act, voted by Congress in 1919, was to be applied after
a delay of eight days. Nazimova seized the telephone and
invited all her friends to come next day for a cocktail. We
attended, Herbert and I, and were very gay when we started
homeward after midnight.

In Venice, a fashionable beach not far from Hollywood, an old rotting hull of a boat lay on the beach. An intelligent restaurateur transformed it into a bar, restaurant, ballroom especially reserved for movie people. There we decided to pass the last night of legal libation. By dawn I was, I think, the only one to have stayed sober...not by virtue, but by taste. I detest alcohol, apart from an occasional cocktail.

One anecdote, among a hundred: A couple struck with love ran to waken the "coroner" (justice of the peace), signed all the necessary papers, found a minister somewhere who blessed them. Waking next morning, their wits recovered, they recalled that they had been married already, and had no other recourse but to run to Reno to get divorced. The law doesn't joke about bigamy.

Those were the great days of moonshine stills, whisky glasses disguised as milk glasses; adulterated alcohol that caused all sorts of damage, smugglers, gangsters. The State soon found that the cure was worse than the disease.

At the moment of closing the description of that beautiful country I am struck by crowding memories, but I fear to tire the reader.

It was now that I received a letter from my lawyer and one from [Joseph] Borries [of the U.S. Amusement Company] asking me to make at least one visit to Fort Lee. I found kind, faithful Borries at his post, happy to see me but very changed.

"Ah, Madame," he told me, "Come back. Defend yourself. They'll leave you nothing but the eyes to weep."

He told me how M.S., the bank representative, stole all the interesting furniture (we had some very good things bought at auction; among others, two beautiful Elizabethan chairs that many decorators had borrowed to copy, a whole set of Empire furniture, etc.).

"Mr. Blaché has lost interest in everything" he told me. "He has refused a rental which was modest enough but which would have allowed you to pay the taxes. The two little companies to whom he sublet the photographic studios have both had fires and the insurance company flatly refuses to pay for the damage."

In short, everything went from bad to worse.

It was then that a producer made me a rather prepos-
terous proposal.

"Put fifty thousand dollars in the business and we'll
give you the direction of Tarzan of the Apes.

At the thought of guiding the acrobatics of that colos-
sal ape-man my blood froze. Happily it was out of the question: I didn't have fifty thousand dollars.

America, they say, always takes back everything she
gives you. Completely discouraged I resolved to return to
France with my children.

After a few weeks of rest, leaving the children in the
care of their grandmother, I knocked on several studio doors
which, of course, were closed to me.

Then I went to Nice where I had some banking friends
who were interested in the Victorine studios. They asked me
to give them my opinion on the installations. I found the
lighting mediocre, the stage sets stored too far away so that
they needed too much time to be transported. Finally, the
tenants deserted the Cote d'Azur for the German studios, in
spite of the neighboring sea and the fine climate. Why?

They asked me to travel to England, since I knew the
language, and to try and find out the cause of this desertion.
I agreed.

In London I met many Americans whom I knew and who
were settling there. They told me that at the Victorine
Studios, in Nice, one could not order a simple fiacre, a sand-
wich, a beer, without having to pay a surcharge. The stage
decors were never ready when they were wanted. The extras were often unreasonable. They employed many White
Russians who still had decent wardrobes, but who exacted
special consideration.

On my return I was offered the direction of the studios,
if I would pay a lot of money. Alas, I had none. Or perhaps the direction of just the extras, for eight-hundred francs
a month? I refused.

Thanks to a friend, I succeeded in collaborating on a feminine revue. I wrote some little stories, tales for children, translations, etc.

In the papers of their deceased father, Raymond and Louis Gaumont have found the report that he had asked of me and had promised to publish in the next edition of the company history, reserving for me, he said, the place which was due to me. Alas, his death prevented this.

Louis Gaumont asked me for permission to use these notes for a lecture he intended to make at the photographic society. I willingly gave it. He made this lecture before the Photographic Society of which I have often spoken, and again I was recognized [on December 8, 1954].

René Jeanne who had himself published so many interesting studies came to see me. He was convinced, and since then has never ceased showing me a thousand proofs of his interest.

It is a failure; is it a success? I don't know.

I lived an intensely interesting life for twenty-eight years. If sometimes my memories make me a little melancholy I remember the words of Roosevelt: "It is hard to have failed, it is worse to have never tried."

EPILOGUE

by Simone Blaché

In 1922, completely discouraged by the collapse of her movie-
making undertaking, following heavy losses my father had
made on the stock exchange in 1918, and after a divorce which
had been for her an extremely painful experience, my mother
naturally thought of returning to France to be near her family. Her divorce had granted her custody of her children
and alimony to help raise them. One of her sisters who lived
in Nice invited us to spend some time with her. Mother accepted, and we liked the city so much that we spent ten
years there, during which mother tried twice to re-enter the
motion picture world, the first time as studio manager of the
Victorine Studios in Nice. At that time the project failed.
It was taken up later with good deal of success, but mother
was not part of it. Her second try, also without success for
her, was as manager of a motion picture center in London in
which Lord Beaverbrook, the newspaper magnate, had an
interest. She went to see him in this connection in London
in 1926 or 1927, I believe. At that time, she also worked
on several scenarios, one of which was Eugenie Grandet,
adapted from Balzac's novel. She tried, again unsuccessfully,
to gather funds to finance these productions, but this was
not a good period in which to seek financial backing for films.
The international economy was on the verge of a grave crisis.

We became poor as mother gradually sold her belongings
--books, paintings, jewelery, and furs -- and father's ability
to meet alimony payments dimished to almost nothing, with
the rate of exchange for the dollar decreasing daily.

By devoting herself completely to her children, becoming cook, cleaning-woman and seamstress, mother was able
to perform the almost impossible task of raising two teenagers,
with very few if any privations, until they were able to start
earning their own livings.

As a result of the very poor economic conditions pre-
valent in Nice at the time, we decided to go to Paris. I left
my job as secretary in a bank and we departed. My mother
still had a few friends in the motion picture world, and
through them, both my brother and I found jobs. Being
American and fluent in both English and French helped, and
for the next eight years I was employed by two different
American film distribution companies.

My mother, in order to add a little to my low starting
wages, tried her hand at writing a few children's stories and
short stories. In 1936 she was able to find a publishing
company, Offenstadt, which published the stories as well as
short résumés of the films, in the form of romances, in a
magazine titled Le Film Complet.

Finally, in 1939, what became known as World War II
was declared. The German invasion followed a year later.
In May of 1940, the company where I worked decided to move
its headquarters to Bordeaux with a reduced staff, and I was
left without a job. A friend of my brother, who worked at
the American Embassy, found a temporary job for me with
an important American publication, the offices of which were
closed by order of the German authorities after a couple of
months. Just prior to that time I received a telephone call
from my brother's friend telling me that a job was open at
the Embassy, if I wished to apply. I rushed to the Embassy,
and that was the beginning of a long and fruitful career with
the foreign service. I was transferred to Vichy, France, with
my mother in 1941, and at the end of the year again transferred, with mother, to Switzerland, where we spent the war
years and mother started work on her memoirs.

From Switzerland, in company of mother, I was transferred to Paris in 1947, to Washington, D.C., in 1952, and
again to Paris in 1955. During our stay in Washington,
mother attempted to trace some of her many films, but her
search was unsuccessful.

In 1955, in Paris, thanks to the efforts of Léon Gaumont's son, Louis, film historian and journalist René Jeanne,
and Henri Langlois of the Cinémathèque Française, I believe,
mother's work as a pioneer of French motion pictures was
marked by the award of the Legion of Honor, an award to
which she was particularly sensitive.

She came with me in 1958 when I was transferred to Brussels. We spent six very happy years there. Her name was finally recognized, thanks to her own efforts, and saved from almost certain oblivion. She was at that time constantly called upon for interviews with film historians and reporters. She appeared in interviews on Belgian and French television.

Mother's active life continued unabated until, at the age of ninety, she suffered a stroke from which she recovered without apparent after-effects. But her physician told me that it was probable she would be the victim of further strokes.

It was then I decided to retire in order to devote myself to her last years. Mother seemed completely recovered when we flew to the United States. Shortly after we had settled in our new home, however, a bad fall and concussion caused a setback from which she never recovered completely. From that time on her physical and mental health deteriorated rapidly. After having resisted the doctor's advice for two years, I had to give in and place her in a convalescent home in New Jersey, where she died on March 24, 1968.

Having lived with her all my life, I would like to add a personal note. Mother was of an ardent and generous nature, youthful and exceptionally energetic. Her mind was open and always curious about scientific or literary novelties. Her deep love of nature and her enthusiasm for life were contagious. For me, she was more a friend than a mother and I owe her the greater part of my happiness.

Appendix A

A REMEMBRANCE

by Madame Olga Petrova

(The following was contained in an undated letter
to Anthony Slide, written in the early seventies)

Alice Guy Blaché was my first director in my first picture
made under a contract for one film to be made by Popular
Plays and Players. Mr. Lawrence Weber was its President.
I believe the title was The Tigress. Mr. Aaron Hoffman was
the author. This was in 1915.

I had met her and her husband, Mr. Herbert Blaché,
at Mr. Weber's office. I liked them both but I was instinc-
tively drawn to her. Had I been asked then WHY? The
answer would have been simple, direct, WHY NOT?

Knowing nothing of the methods of motion picture making, including directors, the idea of their sex didn't occur
to me. If it had I might have reasoned that Mr. Weber being
an astute business man would not have risked losing the substantial profits he counted on me, a neophyte, if he had not
recognized Madame Blaché a reliable, competent director, perfectly capable of protecting his interests. Anyhow, I asked
if she might direct me, and was told she would be pleased to
do so.

As I lived on Long Island, quite a distance from the
studio at Fort Lee, New Jersey, which entailed ferrying my
chauffeur, automobile and me across the Hudson River, 8.30
a.m. was fixed as my daily arrival there, subject to calls
Mr. Lee Shubert might have for me under a contract with
him.

A few weeks later at 8.30 a.m. precisely I reported at

Fort Lee ready for initiation into the Magic, Mystery, ART
and CRAFT of the moving picture business.

Madame Blaché greeted me warmly. She introduced me
to my co-workers of the day and to the cameraman by name.
She showed me my dressing room. A vase of beautiful flowers
welcomed me from the dressing table. She asked if I would
like my lunch brought to me. She consulted me as to the
menu, and so on. In later days she would occasionally meet
with me there for a little cup of black after-lunch coffee, and
interesting, pleasant conversation. The dresses I had brought
were commented upon. I may say here that in those days
wardrobe had to be furnished by the player, NOT the company. This was a considerable expense since one could not
repeat any article of dress in any succeeding film.

These details having been attended to, Madame led me
to the set. When the story had been sent to and read by
me I had voiced surprise that no dialogue or action was included in it. Mr. Weber assured me that all this would be
meticulously attended to later. It was. But in no way did
it resemble anything I could have imagined it would.

Instead Madame vocally outlined what each episode was
about with words and action -- pantomime appropriate to the
situation.

Of course, dialogue, pantomime, as practiced in the
theatre, before audiences, individuals of which could see and
hear from their various seats in the auditorium was one thing,
but to portray them before the single, uncompromising eye of
the camera lens was quite a different proposition. This discomfitted me.

I noticed immediately that my co-workers wore a make-
up much darker than mine, almost a deep beige, whereas I
wore the usual light Leichner's 1-1/2. This discomfitted me
still further, but as Madame Blaché made no comment on it,
neither did I.

I was shown the camera or cameras. I had been photo-
graphed in private studios by professional photographic artists
but these cameras filled me with near terror. They appeared
much taller, much bulkier than any I had seen. They seemed
to resemble fearsome monsters from outer space. However...

Rehearsals started. In the first scene, as in all succeeding ones, Madame Blaché outlined vocally what each episode was about with action, words appropriate to the situation. If the first or second rehearsal pleased her, even
though a player might intentionally or not alter her instruc-
tions, as long as they didn't hurt the scene, even possibly
improve it, she would allow this to pass. If not she would
rehearse and rehearse until they did before calling camera.
When she had cause to correct a player, she would do this
courteously, and in my case, which was more than often,
she might resort to her native tongue. This gentle gesture
touched me deeply, softened any embarrassment I might feel.

After all scenes set for the day had been shot, the
close-ups followed. These I found very difficult. The heat
of the unguarded Klieg lights made one's eyes weep, one's
skin burn, one's hair bristle. However they were part of
one's obligations and so to be obeyed.

These concluded, Madame looked, and was, tired. But
during rehearsals and shooting she never lost dignity nor
poise. She wore a silken glove, but she would have been
perfectly capable of using a mailed fist if she considered it
necessary. This I never saw her do, either on the first day
nor any other day while she directed me. She never bellowed
through the megaphone as I was told many another director
was wont to do. She obtained her results earning the respect
and obedience of her artists. In the four succeeding pictures
she never deviated from these methods.

Unfortunately I never met nor knew Madame, nor any
other of my co-workers outside the studio. When work for
the day was over I hurried back to husband, home and
hearth as quickly as I could -- and BED not long afterwards.

I suppose The Tigress pleased the public, and so Mr.
Weber and Popular Plays and Players, since they offered me
a contract covering a period of three years, albeit at a higher
salary and again subject to plans Mr. Shubert might have for
me. Madame Blaché directed me in the first four under that
aegis. They were, as I remember, The Heart of a Painted
Woman, My Madonna, What Will People Say, and a story the
name of which I don't remember, but was retitled as The
Vampire for release. I am quite sure that if the last named
had come to me under that title I could never have been

presumptuous enough to attempt to interpret it. The realm
of the Vampire character had been created for and royally
queened over by Theda Bara, and I would no more have attempted to emulate her in such roles that I would those of
an Ophelia either.

With the exception of <u>What Will People Say</u>, the play by
Rupert Hughes, they were authored by Aaron Hoffman; though
<u>What Will People Say</u> he adapted for the screen. Why Madame
Blaché didn't continue to direct me after these four I don't
know, but I do know I missed her sorely. I only hope she
found greener pastures. She probably did. Looking back
again I retain for her the same reactions of deep affection
and respect as I had for her so many years ago.

Appendix B

HERBERT BLACHÉ: A BIOGRAPHICAL SKETCH

Although not a major figure in silent film history with none
of his films discussed in any of the standard texts and few
even surviving, Herbert Blaché did direct a number of major
personalities. He directed Alla Nazimova in The Brat (1919)
and Stronger Than Death (1920, which he co-directed with
Charles Bryant); he directed Ethel Barrymore in The Divorcée
(1919); and he directed Buster Keaton in The Saphead (1920).
It was Herbert Blaché who guided Mary Astor at the start of
her career, directing the actress in two short subjects, The
Beggar Maid (1921) and The Young Painter (1922). At the
same time, it should be noted that much of Blaché's career
was spent in directing minor actresses such as Florence Reed,
Emily Stevens and Catherine Calvert.

Herbert Blaché-Bolton (to use his full name) was born
in London on October 5, 1882, of a French father and an
English mother. He was educated in France, and because of
his fluency in various languages he was hired by the London
office of Gaumont to take care of its affairs in various Con-
tinental cities. He and Alice Guy were married in 1907, and
that same year came to the United States, at which time the
couple dropped "Bolton" from their name.

Alice Guy discusses her husband's work in the autobiography. In the Twenties, Herbert Blaché remarried. He
was a contract director at Universal from 1923-1926, handling
minor features starring Gladys Walton, Herbert Rawlinson and
others. Blaché ended his directorial career in 1929 with the
Universal feature, Burning the Wind, starring Hoot Gibson
and Virginia Brown Faire, which he co-directed with Henry
MacRae. He died in Santa Monica, California, on October 23,
1953.

One of the few contemporary authors to write of Herbert

Blaché is Robert Grau. In his The Theatre of Science, published in 1914 Grau comments,

> Few men in the photo-drama art are as well equipped
> to grapple with the problems of silent drama produc-
> tion as Herbert Blaché...Herbert Blaché is as much
> at home writing a scenario, editing a picture drama,
> cutting and titling a photoplay, or directing big
> spectacular scenes of a pretentious multiple-reel
> feature as he is managing the affairs of two large
> flourishing producing companies and acting as presi-
> dent of the Exclusive Supply Corporation, with his
> sensitive fingers continually upon the active pulse
> of the whole motion picture market, both in this
> country and abroad.

In the same issue of The Moving Picture World -- July
11, 1914 -- in which his wife wrote on a woman's place in
photoplay production, Herbert Blaché discussed "The Life of
a Photodrama." The last major reference to Blaché is in
Carolyn Lowrey's The First One Hundred Noted Men and Wom-
en of the Screen, published in 1920. Interestingly this book,
although written by a woman, has no place for Alice Guy, and
she is not even mentioned in the full-page article on her husband. Even films which she directed are credited as her husband's productions.

Appendix C

MADAME ALICE BLACHÉ

by H.Z. Levine

Little Magda Foy, the "Solax Kid," once came flying into Madame Blaché's office, and in a lisping, tearful voice exclaimed: "Oh, Madame, can't you make them stop teasing me? I don't want to be called Billy, and that's what they all call me. Please tell them not to call me Billy." Madame looked up from a scenario she was preparing, turned in her chair to face little Magda and with a smile kindly asked, "Who is teasing you?"

"They aw-aw-all are. There's Mr. [Billy] Quirk, and Mr. [Darwin] Karr, and Mr. [Lee] Beggs, and the rest. I won't have it." And like a big, willful girl, Magda stamped her foot in protest. Madame straightened out a bow which had gone awry in Magda's hair, soothingly patted her curls, and told "the kid" to tell her annoyers that they were to submit themselves to having their ears boxed. Magda gleefully danced out of the office, after hugging her rescuer. With an amused twinkle, Madame turned back to resume the work of preparing her manuscript for production.

Before very long Madame was again interrupted. This time some one sent in his card. He asked for a place as a director. She spoke to him about pictures and their production, about the public's taste and the exhibitors' demands. The visitor was of the opinion that the public would take to anything foisted on them in the shape of a moving picture. He was wrong. She spoke to him just long enough, without being abrupt. She had him "sized up" and then arose, and thus terminated the interview, deciding in her own mind that the applicant "would not do."

Before Madame had an opportunity to resume her work,

the telephone bell rang and a voice told her her presence was immediately needed at the factory. Before she had time to step out of her office, one of the directors put his head into the doorway and asked if "Madame would please come to the studio so that he might have her opinion on a scene then being taken." As it was impossible for her to do two things at once, she nodded, and first systematically solved the problem at the factory and then gave a puzzled director the benefit of her advice and long experience.

These are all incidental to her day's work. It is the atmosphere in which she works all day long. Once Madame, in a moment of exhaustion, said -- still with a smile -- "If it was possible to divide myself in ten it would still not be enough. It is Madame here and Madame there. Madame is wanted everywhere." From 9 in the morning until 6 or 7 in the evening Madame Blaché is on the job.

She quietly moves about the plant, unostentatiously and unobtrusively energetic. She carries with her an air of refinement and culture, and her dark, modest clothes bespeak and emphasize her dignity. This dignity, however, never borders on frigidity. She smiles encouragingly upon every one she meets. Her commands are executed to the letter with dispatch and efficiency, not because she is feared, but because she is liked. Although Madame has decided ideas, and at times will obstinately insist that they be carried out, she is always only too willing to listen to suggestions. She is not a woman who is amenable to flattery. Unlike other women in business, she is really the first sometimes to see her own errors and will often, without resentment, admit the justice of criticism.

Madame Blaché is a striking example of the modern woman in business who is doing a man's work. She is doing successfully what men are trying to do. She is succeeding in a line of work in which hundreds of men have failed. Ask Madame that question which interviewers just "do to death" -- "To what do you attribute your success, Madame?" and she will look (as she always does look) straight at you out of slate-colored eyes and reply only with a characteristic shrug of the shoulders and a little twinkle of the eye, which means that she hasn't analyzed her success.

Madame Blaché, being thoroughly artistic, having been born

and bred in an artistic environment, always demands the very
highest artistic values from her directors and actors. Sometimes what she in Paris would have considered classic art,
the Board of Censors here insist is objectionable. Madame
cannot reconcile Parisien training with American prudishness.
While on this subject one day she vehemently expressed herself in this fashion:

> In France all artists aspire to get realism. The
> more realistic, the more like the realities of life are
> our creations, the more pleased the public and the
> more emphatic is our artistic triumph. Here, con-
> trary to all established precedents of art, we find
> conditions such that the showing of a revolver or
> the jimmying of a desk or the cracking of a safe is
> objectionable. Such a point of view is primitive. I
> believe, as others, that the flagrant exhibition of
> crime and the glorification of vice are a menace to
> society; but the exhibition of crime to bring home a
> moral lesson with a dramatic climax, and the achieve-
> ment of a period in the true development of a char-
> acter, should be permissible. Pantomime is the most
> difficult form of expression, and to limit it to mere
> namby-pamby, milk-and-water themes manacles its
> chances of development in this country.

During the day's work Madame Blaché comes in direct
personal contact with all the intricacies of her establishment.
She is in close touch with her affairs, and, indeed, she is
the center from which radiates all Solax activities.

-- Photoplay, Vol. II, No. 2,
March 1912, p. 37-38.

Appendix D

STUDIO SAUNTERINGS

by Louis Reeves Harrison

In approaching a studio or an office you may find yourself
dealing with a raw specimen of humanity at the outset--you
can make up your mind there and then that you will come
upon some half-baked ones further on. And the contrary is
true. If you are treated with courtesy and consideration from
the outset as I was when I sauntered over to the Solax studio
at Flushing, you can count upon it that some one of enlighten-
ment and superior breeding is high in control of affairs. In
this case, the head of the business, the originator of it, the
capitalist, the art director, the chief working director, is a
refined French woman, Madame Alice Blaché.

This is woman's era, and Madame Blaché is helping to
prove it without making any fuss at all. She only favors
universal suffrage when satisfied that women are ready for
it, and she is so modest about what she had done in the
Gaumont and Solax companies that I had to depend upon others
for any details relating to her remarkable career in the production of moving pictures. Modesty is the most endearing
quality woman ever shows to man, egotism being his specialty
and most pronounced characteristic, and along with it the
head of the Solax Company exhibits a delighful composure of
manner under all circumstances, no matter how trying. The
average business man imagines that he enhances his importance
by exhibiting that enemy of politeness, haste, as if the tre-
mendous responsibility of making a living kept him in a state
of constant high pressure. I have been in studios where
there was no inherent lack of appreciation of the value of
publicity, but those in control assume that old you'll-have-to-
excuse-me air, as though a momentary diversion of energy
would cause the entire commercial structure to collapse, and
those men of small ability to meet contingencies are the first

to complain that they are never able to attract attention. At
the Solax, I was personally conducted by gentle-mannered
Levine, editor of The Magnet, and so well treated from start
to finish that my work became a pleasure. Levine realized
that I was not at the studio as an individual, but as the representative of the only periodical generally regarded as an
established authority on moving pictures in this country. He
is a live wire.

From Levine, and from others, I learned that Madame
Alice Blaché became associated with the Gaumont Company
very early in the game, when Mr. Gaumont was absorbed with
the scientific department of production or merely engaged in
photographing moving objects. She inaugurated the presentation of little plays on the screen by that company some six-
teen or seventeen years ago, operating the camera, writing
or adapting the photodramas, setting the scenes and handling
the actors. I had an opportunity to see how efficient she was
in her diversity of roles before the day was over and was
amazed at her skill, especially in directing the action of a
complicated scene. She came to this country in 1907--her
husband then being general manager of the Gaumont Company
in America--and established an entirely independent organization, having no connection with the older one, and launched
it successfully as the Solax Company.

When I reached the present studio--a new one is in
process of construction across the Hudson in New Jersey--
Madame Blaché and a large body of actors and actresses had
gone some distance into sylvan scenes of Long Island for the
purpose of producing in the sunlight several acts of Fra Diavolo, a large photodrama adapted from Auber's opera of the
same name. I went immediately to the base of operations in
an automobile with Levine and came upon a fully-equipped
stage set up in the open, with Madame Blaché conducting rehearsals from an elevated camera platform.

The scene from the south was an inn interior, presumably that of L'Hôtellerie de Terracine, but it was a two-faced
arrangement, the north side representing the entrance of the
hostelry. From within one could look out into the open and
note the approach on horseback of the famous Calabrian ban-
dit (Billie Quirk in this instance), and his action at the entrance could be depicted from either an exterior or from an
interior point of view, a most ingenious disposition of the

entire structure. On the stage at the moment was jovial
George Paxton in the role of a richard, a pompous gentleman
of wealth, with sedussante Miss Simpson as his young and
attractive wife and inn loungers, all seated at tables, while
picturesque waiters and waitresses, fresh from the opera,
enlivened the effect with their gay costumes.

The entire group was a glowing palette of color, a
bright and warm costume treatment against an interesting
background, with an especially well designed fireplace as the
striking decorative feature, but the thing calculated to make
us forget the theater was the glimpse of nature through the
open door of the inn. There is an abundance of movement
in the scene, which becomes intensified when innkeeper Foy
announces to his servants that another traveler is in sight.
Sure enough, there is Billie Quirk in the title role riding up
to the entrance from the near distance. There is a stir over
his entrance; the young wife notices the handsome stranger;
the elderly husband regards the newcomer contemptuously;
Fra Fiavolo orders refreshments and the action becomes extremely complicated, especially in the small scope of the foreground where the principals are gathered.

It is to be expected that Fannie Simpson, Billie Quirk
and George Paxton will carry on their parts with intelligence
and harmony of relation, but there are a half dozen or more
others to fit in and not complicate matters; the director's
eyes have to be everywhere. Madame Blaché gives her sig-
nals with as much ease and composure as though there had
been a month of dress rehearsals. She is never ruffled,
never agitated; never annoyed by the obtrusive efforts of
minor characters to thrust themselves into prominence. With
a few simple directions, uttered without apparent emotion,
she handles the interweaving movements like a military leader
might the maneuvers of an army. "I like American actors and
actresses" she said brightly; "they are so willing to do as
they are told and take such a live interest in what they are
doing."

I was surprised to hear her say that--every little girl
and boy in France seems to be born with the dramatic instinct.
"Are they as good as the French?" I asked. "Quite as good."
she assured me, "and so much more pliable. It is pleasure
to train them." The secret of it lies in her own sweetness
of manner and inexhaustible patience. I could have hurled

several two-edged epithets at a waiter who kept thrusting into the main action. The directress has that essence of politeness, a very kind heart. She accomplished gently what a
man would attempt by stinging sarcasm. I could not help re-
calling what the distinguished British statesman, orator and
writer, Edmund Burke, once said.

"Manners are more important than laws. They vex or
soothe, barbarize or refine us, by the constant and insen-
sible operation of the air we breathe. They give form and
color to our lives."

Rehearsal of the interior scenes had been concluded,
the detached platform was occupied by Madame Blaché, the
camera man and myself, there was some talk of adjourning
for lunch, when the wildest kind of a scene was enacted before our eyes, only a few feet from the structure to be photo-
graphed. Some horses attached to an old-fashioned stage had
been standing unattended in the sunlight when they took
fright and dashed straight for the prospective stage of Fra
Diavolo's misdeeds. They started another unattached team of
horses, became entangled in an uprearing and mad struggle,
stagehands and actors in costume dashed into the perilous
situation, and it looked as though a vast amount of damage
would shortly result. With all that going on the camera man
stood inactive where a newspaper photographer would have
used every reel in his machine. Perhaps he was afraid to
use the moving-picture camera, as it was not his own, but a
more animated picture could not have been prepared.

One team finally escaped and made a bee line for the
spot where a number of performers, including little Magda
[Foy] and her mother, were sitting while waiting their turns
or watching the rehearsal, veered from this fatal course, and
ran away toward Flushing. The bed of a moving picture
actor is not always one of roses. The company sought a
shady nook, and I asked the enterprising camera man to snap
a shot at a picturesque group of principals gathered together
under the trees--they were occupied in appeasing the never-
failing professional appetite. I now had opportunity of renewing acquaintance with the tiniest tot of three, who appeared in The Little Major.

Little Magda has improved to such an extent since she
appeared with Helen Anderson In The Little Major--she could

barely toddle through her part then--that she has become an
accomplished actress. She was a comical baby then, though
very pretty, and she gave no signs of possessing histrionic
ability--it was all we could do to make her keep her eyes
shut when she was supposed to be asleep. I was amazed,
therefore, when I watched her act on the Solax stage a few
weeks ago, to see her perform with intelligence and feeling
far beyond her tender years. This remarkable change is
probably due to an unusual environment, both her mother
and her father appearing regularly in the photodrama.

Magda's parents keep her strong and healthy--off stage
she is nothing but a sturdy, romping child--and they do not
deplete her energy by shutting her up in some ill-ventilated
school. Yet she is brighter than most kidlets of her age and
is building the physical strength in this formative period that
she will need later on in life. She has an ability that grown-
ups often lack, that of concentrating her attention upon what
she is doing while the picture of her movements is being
taken--she can fix her mind upon the subject in hand better
than many mature women--and seems to act correctly in a
difficult situation from instinct. This serious work has not
in the least spoiled the little girl. She is simply a happy
child of tender heart and strong natural affections, more like
a restless and vigorous little boy than a repressed girl, and
her conduct is just as natural as if she had never played
some difficult leading roles. She is what children should be.

After lunch in the woods came the actual performance
of part of <u>Fra Diavolo</u> as it will appear on the screen. It
always sets me on edge, like a close ring fight or anxious
game of ball, to watch the performers in action while the moving picture is being taken. The smallest error may result
in doing the entire scene over again, there is a feeling of
suspense like that awakened by old-fashioned melodrama, when
it looks as though the heroine would get her head sawed off,
and one experiences relief when all turns out well. To re-
press my excitement I fastened my attention upon a string of
garlic hanging in this Italian inn, supposedly to give it "atmosphere," and waited. There was only one slip. That
same waiter obtruded where he was not required and the
whole scene had to be done over again from the beginning.

I was glad to see Madame Blaché insist upon good conduct among members of her company--this she did firmly,

though her methods are invisible--for actors are not particularly strong on manners. Only recently it was asserted by a
prominent New York manager that not an actor in this city
could conduct himself on the stage, not even walk across it,
like a plain ordinary gentleman. Old Socks-and-Buskin is
still fond of spats and the matinee idol cannot leave his silk
hat home when he goes to the country. In moving picture
companies there is a tendency to play to the camera, which
robs a performance of intense effect.

In a highly emotional photodrama I should like to see
the performers enter more deeply into the spirit of the story,
express as closely as possible the vexations and petty anxi-
eties of actual existence more than they do. These are quite
as effective as murderous glances out the corners of eyes or
copious weeping in moments of sorrow. Thousands of people
show fortitude in trial or trouble, though the suppressed
emotion may leave its character traces on the countenance.
The great idea is to indicate clearly though delicately what is
passing in the mind at an intense moment, and this can be
best done by feeling as the character would under the circumstances.

I would like very much to have a woman of such exceptional taste as the head of the Solax Company make a
study of our beautiful country homes from both an outer and
an inner point of view, not the pitiful humbug that goes on
at watering places. The esthetic tendency of American women
has been highly cultivated during the last ten or fifteen years
by really wonderful periodicals such as Country Life, devoted
to describing successful homes with illustrations of correct
interiors. The photodramas show absolutely none of these
except when taken in Los Angeles, and the selections there
seem to be made at random.

A Frenchman will easily set a French interior--that is
largely a question of periods--and the same is true of a cultivated English director, but our audiences are compelled to
look at veritable abortions for our own settings--they look as
though they came from a second-hand store or junk shop--
and this is so offensive that many of the best people are
driven from the little theaters by the hideous and repulsive
furniture and drapings of "home" interiors. Correct scenes,
representatively American in the best sense of the word,
would greatly enhance any brand of moving pictures both

here and abroad. It must be remembered that the visual appeal is all in all, these are <u>pictures</u>, and to have great power
they must be consistent.

Cheap-looking colonials have been used to the point of
nausea, and as it would not be possible to enter the true
American houses where dinners, dances and week's-end parties
are given in a brilliant social atmosphere, the surest guide
can only be found in the great periodicals given over to il-
lustrating the delightful interior life of American people. The
fresh and original beauty of these homes would contribute
tremendously to the charm of moving pictures and give the
first producer of them a Tiffany-like standing in this country
and abroad.

I was loathe to leave Madame Blaché and her happy
family of brave men and fair women, but the declining sun
reminded me that I had a long journey before me, and we
poor scribes have to do our work at all hours, so I reluc-
tantly said goodbye. I was, however, cheered on my way
by the last words of sweet little Magda:

"When r'you comin' again?"

                    -- The Moving Picture World,
                       Vol. XII, No. 11, June 15,
                       1912, p. 1007-1011.

Appendix E

It has been your privilege to know something of the ups and
downs of the film business, you who read the ever recurring
numbers of this particular brand of yellow-backed journal,
and you will be surprised to know that with it is identified
a real, for sure woman. This woman, because she had dared
to follow her own pleasure into the mysterious realm of moto-
graphy, becomes at once more interesting than her sisters
who merely contribute toward the making. Madam Alice Blaché
Blaché, president and general manager, director and producer, makes films. Get that; she makes 'em. There isn't
any part of the game she doesn't know. She started early,
but she lays no claim of being "the oldest man in the business!"

In the preface to A Prodigal Father, Alexandre Dumas,
fils. said: "Of all the various forms of thought, the stage
is that which nearest approaches the plastic arts, inasmuch
as we cannot work in it, unless we know its material processes; but with this difference--that in the other arts one
learns these processes, while in play-writing one guesses
them; or to speak more accurately; they are in us to begin
with." What a pity Dumas might not have written of motion
pictures, instead of the mastery of his father's talent. He
adds, in the next sentence--"One can become a painter, a
sculptor, a musician, by sheer study--one does not become a
dramatic author in this fashion. A caprice of nature makes
your eye in such a way that you can see a thing after a particular manner--not absolutely correct, but which must, nevertheless, appear to any other persons that you wish to have
so think, the only correct point of view." Here we have a
statement, pertinent to the production of motion pictures.
There is no more wonderful a personage than the producer
of the motion-picture play--the judge of the scenario; the

scientist of optics; the silence; the gesture; the entrancing
atmospheric combinations--the producers of modern films for
exhibition purposes "is born--and made"; there can be no
mistake about it.

The biography of Madam Alice Blaché will be written
some day. It might be written in a dozen lines, so simple,
so tranquil, so fortunate has been her life, in-so-far as we
are to know, judging from a limited knowledge of it. Madame
Blaché was born in France, inheriting her good looks from
her parents, who were accomplished enough to fit their daughter for higher education. She lived in a household of culture,
good breeding and healthy fun. She can easily lay claim to
all that constitutes a clever woman; full of epigram and humor
in conversation. That she combines the requisites of business
is best emphasized by her rather extraordinary position as
the dominant figure in her factory and studio, engaging in a
peculiarly hazardous occupation. One of the notable charms
of this exceptional woman is her abundance of balance and
common-sense. If she has a temper, it is always under control.

Madame Blaché associated with the Gaumont Company in
Paris, when it first engaged in film-making. Her ability, dem-
onstrated through the years of service in all departments of
the great plant, won for her the full confidence of the officers. When she married Herbert Blaché, she came to America
as the dutiful wife and counselor of Gaumont's representative
in this country. She was quick to see the possibilities of an
independent plant and with her own money, she organized
The Solax Company; built the establishment on a plot of
ground joining the Gaumont works at Flushing, L.I.; assumed
the presidency, gathered about her the talent required and
superintended and managed every detail. It was only recently
that the concern vacated the old quarters to occupy a larger,
more modern place erected at Ft. Lee, N.J.

Most film folks are familiar with the Solax brand. It is
identified with the Film Supply Company program and with
new and modern facilities behind it, combined with the fitness
of Madame Blaché, a still better product will follow.

It is unnecessary to give the lady's age--this is not a
biography. The family bible is across the ocean, but don't
you recall that there was a little Blaché who came to live at

Flushing, last summer, and can you imagine that with Papa
as president of the Film Supply, and Mamma as the president
of Solax, the Baby will grow up and not file his application for
a license with the Patents Company?

Madame Blaché has very little patience with the film
censors.   She is French and believes in realism.   She argues
that the public should be the judge.   No one knows better
than she, that pantomime is beset with plenty of troubles at
best and that censorship of realistic scenes adds to the producer's burden.   Her foreign training and the knowledge of
what would "go" abroad has been the innocent cause of an
occasional shock when she tried to bring home a strong moral
lesson.   But at that, cleverness and a record of meeting
every situation face to face, has made the Madame great and
that the Solax guiding star is a woman seems to be lost in
the hurly-burly of business.

                        -- Motography, Vol. VIII, No.
                        8, October 12, 1912, p. 293-
                        294.

ALICE BLACHÉ, A DOMINANT
FIGURE IN PICTURES

by Harvey H. Gates

Madame Alice Blaché was busy at that moment. Would I not
wait, or perhaps I would be pleased to go up into the studio
where the Madame was occupied in supervising the production
of several scenes in a film comedy soon to be released? It
was the opportunity I sought--to watch this remarkable woman at work--and on expressing my wish. I was led through
a hall and up a stairway, perfumed strongly with fresh paint,
warmly greeted, given a chair in the shadows--just outside
of the blinding arc lights, and left to myself to form the
first impressions that I was afterwards to have enlarged and
confirmed in a congenial, personal conversation with her.

Often we hear tales, recounting the wonderful achieve-
ments of green boys from the country who come to the great
metropolis to establish themselves in the world, but seldom
does it fall to the lot of history's pen to record a more striking romance of the business world than the one found in the
life of the woman whom I was now observing. Nine years ago
Madame Balché came to this country as the wife and counselor
of Herbert Blaché, the American representative of the Gaumont
Company. She could not speak a word of English and her
friends could be counted on one hand. Now she stands as
the dominant figure in a motion picture factory and studio
which she organized and built up, from which she draws an
income of from fifty to sixty thousand dollars annually. And
her friends--well, we know that success is productive of unlimited friends.

"Yes," she said to me afterwards, "it is curious that I
should now be engaged in the business of producing pictures,
and yet again it isn't. When I first came to this country, I

entertained no idea of entering the field, though I had been
associated with the Gaumont Company in Paris ever since its
inception. I was ignorant of your language, your customs and
conditions here, and I thought over the matter for some time
before I ventured."

Dame Fate really had little to do with the career of
Madame Blaché. What she has accomplished is solely the result of personal effort, thought and the qualities within her.
The venture was carefully planned, reasoned out and launched
and very little was left to the caprice of chance. In
speaking of this she said: "Waste has always been a terrify-
ing word to me. Waste, I think, in any shape or form, is
one of the greatest of crimes--I abhor it in my own life and
in the lives of others and I guess it was this very thing
which first decided me to act. I had had experience in the
picture business--I knew it thoroughly and it seemed a shame
not to put my knowledge to some good advantage when there
was so much room. My husband was with me heart and soul
and had it not been for his relations with the Gaumont Company, we would have conducted the business together. I
have never been without his advice and support and the support of my many friends.

"Perhaps I should not have been able to accomplish so
much in any other country, particularly in France." This
was a remark which puzzled me and the inquiry to know why,
led to a discussion of conditions and people here and in her
native land. Her opinions are interesting.

"I am a woman. Do you understand?"

Vaguely I did, for I knew and had seen something of
the women and the position they hold in Europe, but I remained unsatisfied until she had spoken further.

"Here, in a general way, the fight and victory is to
the strong, irrespective of sex. It is not so where I came
from. In France we are women, just women, to be treated
with all due deference by the men of breeding and to be
pampered and showered with affection. Women are commonly
in a state of dependence, and are not likely to exercise their
reason with freedom. Art in some forms is practically the
only field open to them. There are exceptions, of course,
but they are rare.

"It is so different here and never for once have I been sorry that my husband brought me with him--to live, to associate and to grow among such nice, cosmopolitan people. They talk of French chivalry. Yes, it does exist, but mostly it is superficial. So long as a woman remains in what they term, her place, she suffers little vexation. Yet let her assume the prerogatives usually accorded to her brothers and she is immediately frowned upon. The attitude towards women in America is vastly different.

"During my first experience with a film stock company in this country, I did not fully realize this and I put into practise wrong tactics. I ruled with an iron hand. I soon learned my mistake and ever since then I have progressed more rapidly. An American gentleman, on joining my company, presumes that I know what I am doing and that I have a right to be where I am. It is a constant conflict when a woman in a French studio attempts to handle and superintend men in their work. They don't like it, and they are not averse to showing their feelings."

It is unnecessary to state that Madame Blaché had had ample occasion to watch and study acting before the camera, here and in her own country, and that she has arrived at some conclusions respecting the subject. Acting, according to her, is a question of the individual to a large extent. Technically, good acting is not relegated to certain kinds of temperaments, or to any particular race of people. The power comes from within and is actuated by the love of approbation. She maintains that players of equal capabilities are often widely different in their natures and mental powers.

"In my studio," she continued. "I say to one of my company, this is your role. He or she takes the manuscript --reads it over--studies it, and reasons out his or her conception of the interpretation. An American's method of playing the part is regulated by the head and as a result, the director, comparatively speaking, has little trouble with him. If his ideas on some points are wrong, a director can usually correct them by an appeal to reason. This, to the average Frenchman, is not acting. Mind, I say to the average. I do not believe that way myself. What difference does it make so long as the same end is realized?

"If interpretation, as it does with the French, comes

spontaneously from the heart, perhaps it may be a trifle more
effective, if that interpretation happens to be correct. Some
times it is incorrect and in such a case, the director is
brought to his wit's end in trying to show the player his mis-
conception. 'I feel it from the soul' is the one expression
from the player used against all the arguments the director
can produce. For that reason it is much harder to work with
my own people than with Americans."

While Madame Blaché was commenting upon her work as
a director and the head of the Solax Film Company, the remark was dropped that not long ago there was an opening in
her company for a director which had remained unfilled for
several months. "Is it then so hard to secure directors?"
I asked, and the answer that followed swerved the conversation to the topic "good, bad and indifferent" people now
employed in the picture business.

"I find it hard," she said, "to get good directors and
I will not burden myself with a bad one. For that reason
the position remained open. You know there are so many
people who profess to know the art when they do not. I am
willing to let the other manufacturers experiment with them.
Perhaps that is selfish of me, for really some one must teach
them. There are some companies that will do this without
realizing it. They imagine they are getting their money's
worth."

"Does that, perchance, answer the question of why
there are so many incompetent people in the business?" I
ventured, and Madame Balché nodded her head in affirmation.

"You see," she continued, "we have not arrived at that
stage where we can appreciate values. The result is, we
have upstarts foisted upon us. Not so much in the acting
branch, however. If the head director knows his business
at all, he can prevent that. But the time was not long since
when we had poor acting as well. It was not our fault though.
The business was not taken seriously and we could only rally
the failures of the profession to our aid. There is absolutely
no excuse now for indifferent acting in a picture."

A biography of Madame Blaché will some day be written
for every one to read the details of her simple, fortunate
life, and here are a few of the facts it will contain. It was

with her own money (not much) that she organized the Solax
Company; built the establishment on a plot of ground ad-
joining the Gaumont works at Flushing, L. I., and with an
eye to her possibilities of doing something of value, she assumed the presidency, gathered about her the talent required
and superintended and managed every detail. It was only
recently that the concern vacated the old quarters to occupy
a larger, more modern place erected at Fort Lee, N.J. And
with it all, she insisted that never has she neglected her
duties as a wife and a mother.

"I am constituted that way," she explained. "While I
love to accomplish big things, I think that my first duty is
to my home."

And her children. There are two of them: Simone, a
precocious little girl of five years and a boy who first opened
his eyes to look upon this world a few months ago. Simone
spends considerable time with her mother. The studio is her
playground and the players--who compare to a big family--
are her playmates. It is on this child, her pranks and her
foolishly wise chatter, that the mother most delights to dwell.

"This girl," laughed Madame Blaché, "she is so funny
some times. Her influence and bright spirits help, in a great
measure, to keep my people satisfied and happy. Seldom does
one of them leave me. None of them have been with me less
than a year. The other night Simone was watching the production of a scene wherein the hero had to die. 'Mamma,'
she said, 'why does Mr. [Darwin] Karr--that is my leading
man--have to die?' 'Because he is poor--he has no money,'
I answered. The next evening while we were going home,
she fumbled in her tiny purse, drew out fifteen cents I had
given her several days previous and said, 'Mamma give this
to Mr. Karr and maybe he won't have to die.' "

What her children will do when they grow up, she does
not pretend to know. She will direct and mould to the best
of her ability, but the choice will be left to them. That is
the prerogative of all children, she believes.

                         -- The New York Dramatic
                         Mirror, Vol. LXVIII, No.
                         1768, November 6, 1912,
                         p. 28.

Appendix G

THE MAKING OF A FEATURE

It was our singular good fortune this week to drop in at the
Solax studio at Fort Lee. The bright sunny building, its
atmosphere of cheerfulness and good fellowship, which even
the least important employees seem to feel and take part in,
and the courtesy of Madame Blaché herself, leave in the visitor's mind at all times, a pleasant memory. Every one who
goes out to Fort Lee comes back enthusiastic and full of admiration. It is not only the agreeableness of the place and
of the people one meets there that one notices, but the
smoothness and the order with which the work is carried on.
There is no litter about and seemingly no hurry; it is the
best kind of a place for good work and very clearly any eye
that can weave a story from small suggestions and foresee a
fine picture from one or two perfect scenes, it is full of the
romance of long ago. For Madame Blaché is working on a
three-reel picture that will tell the grand old story of Dick
Whittington and his cat. We were shown the bells--they are
of good size--that will sing out encouragement to the footsore
lad, "Turn again Whittington, Lord Mayor of London." And
we were also shown other things that made us eager to see
the finished picture in all its three reels.

It will be a better offering even, so Madame Blaché
says, than the Solax Fra Diavolo. If she is not mistaken in
this, it will indeed be something very fine. For our part,
judging by two scenes that we saw being turned, by a reel
of what has already been made and by the absolutely perfect
sets and furniture prepared for the other scenes, we are
sure that it will make a stir on its artistic merits. It was by
no means an easy picture to plan and prepare for, since every
one of its important scenes had to be constructed; the times
of Dick Whittington have passed away. Madame Blaché is not
one who is content, in producing this story, to get back-
grounds that are something like those among which this hero

of at least every English speaking school boy lived; she has
aimed at giving an illusion of reality and it is plain that she
has spared no pains or money in her determination to get
this illusion. In the reels already taken she has reached it
in a most remarkable way. We saw a picture of a big kitchen
in the house of an English merchant, where Dick has obtained
a job as scullion. He had hoped to find gold and be a great
merchant at once. But he has at least found a home though
he has to work; blow the fires with the bellows and polish up
the brass work and pans and pots, all old style, of which
the kitchen is full. The suggestion that this scene gives is
helped much by the acting, but all together, it is full of
reminiscence of old prints and makes us think that we have
seen just such a kitchen and know that the scene is what it
ought to be.

Some of the scenes will need an old time English galleon,
the ship on which the cat makes the voyage that is to prove
so profitable to Dick. This is so well done that we took
pleasure looking it over and noticing its details; it looks like
the real thing and will make a picture worth seeing. Then
there is a picture of the gate of the city at the time Dick
reaches it and where he is stopped by the "Beef Eater" on
guard. This will make one wonder where it was found, for
it has been made to seem massive and looks like stone. To
make these sets, study and research were called for. Before
she began the production, Madame Blaché spent a good many
days looking up old prints and studying the times. Knowing
what was needed, she has gone ahead to obtain it without
regard to expense in reason. That this is so is not only
claimed, but quite apparent. And because of it the offering
will be not only entertaining, but valuable for its instruction.

A poor picture in the best setting possible would be
like a beautiful cup to a thirsty traveler. He might admire
it, but unless it held something to quench his thirst he would
hardly take deep interest in it. This picture will be full of
the truest humanity, as clear as sparkling water. Those
scenes that we saw being played where acted in a thoroughly
sincere and natural way. One comes to realize, while watching Madame Blaché at work with her players, what alertness
and care for smallest things at every instant of a scene is
needed in the making of really good pictures. Standing behind this gifted producer and listening to her quietly given
admonitions to her players, one gets a vivid impression of
what her mind is drawing in its imagination. It seems magi-

cal, the closeness of the understanding between her and the
player who happens to be the center of the story at any
seemingly small part of an instant and it is marvelous that
the effect she desires is obtained so easily. It is the power
of quiet direction attaining its ends. That one feels this influence while watching Madame Blaché at work shows how
sharp and clear-cut is her visualizing power and how thoroughly she knows just what she wants.

While a scene is being turned the studio seems as still
as a mill pond at sunset; and yet, if anything humorous happens, Madame Blaché is the first to see its fun and the first
to laugh. When things happen that spoil the scene even, and
such sometimes bob up anywhere, she is apt to catch the
humor of it. Such an attitude toward life saves much nervous
strain and wear and tear. There were no signs of nerves in
the Solax studio; but we did notice a good deal of modulated
fun and laughter which never interfered with the work. The
admiration and sincere loyalty of all Madame Blaché's artistic
household, is apparent everywhere. Fun is not choked down
and orderly work certainly flourished. In one of the picture's
scenes a mule is needed to draw an old English cart. He is
just an ordinary mule such as can stand on his front legs
alone for the time a steel spring might snap and need no hind
support at all. One of the players wanted to make friends
with his muleship and made overtures to scratch his back.
It looked as though a knife blade had shut and opened and
the friendly man got a cue for his exit after a scene in which
there was no faking.

No estimate of what the players are going to give us
would be fair at this time. There is a large cast and we have
seen only a few of them; but those few have our admiration.
Vinnie Burns is Dick at the time he comes to London and we
are sure that she, in those scenes we saw, will score a big
success, she deserves it anyway. Mrs. Hurley's work is too
well known to need more than a passing notice that it is equal
to the best we have seen from her. That is saying a good
deal in the way of high commendation. Every other player
whose work we noticed seemed to feel the romantic atmosphere
of the story and all filled their parts in perfection or something very near to it.

                              -- The Moving Picture World,
                                 Vol. XV, No. 9, March 1,
                                 1913, p. 873-874.

Appendix H

WOMAN'S PLACE IN PHOTOPLAY PRODUCTION

by Alice Guy Blaché

It has long been a source of wonder to me that many women have not seized upon the wonderful opportunities offered to them by the motion-picutre art to make their way to fame and fortune as producers of photodramas. Of all the arts there is probably none in which they can make such splendid use of talents so much more natural to a woman than to a man and so necessary to its perfection.

There is no doubt in my mind that a woman's success in many lines of endeavor is still made very difficult by a strong prejudice against one of her sex doing work that has been done only by men for hundreds of years. Of course this prejudice is fast disappearing, and there are many vo-cations in which it has not been present for a long time. In the arts of acting, music, painting, and literature, woman has long held her place among the most successful workers, and when it is considered how vitally all of these arts enter into the production of motion pictures, one wonders why the names of scores of women are not found among the successful cre-ators of photodrama offerings.

Not only is a woman as well fitted to stage a photodrama as a man, but in many ways she has a distinct advantage over him because of her very nature and because much of the knowledge called for in the telling of the story and the creation of the stage setting is absolutely within her province as a member of the gentler sex. She is an authority on the emotions. For centuries she has given them full play while man has carefully trained himself to control them. She has developed her finer feelings for generations, while being protected from the world by her male companions, and she is naturally religious. In matters of the heart her superiority

is acknowledged, and her deep insight and sensitiveness in
the affairs of Cupid give her a wonderful advantage in developing the thread of love and plays such an all-important
part in almost every story that is prepared for the screen.
All of the distinctive qualities that she possesses come into
direct play during the guiding of the actors in making their
character drawings and interpreting the different emotions
called for by the story. For to think and to feel the situation demanded by the play is the secret of successful acting,
and sensitiveness to those thoughts and feelings is absolutely
essential to the success of a stage director.

    The qualities of patience and gentleness possessed to
such a high degree by womankind are also of inestimable
value in the staging of a photodrama. Artistic temperament
is a thing to be reckoned with while directing an actor, in
spite of the treatment of the subject in the comic papers,
and a gentle, soft-voiced director is much more conducive
to good work on the part of the performer than the overstern,
noisy tyrant of the studio.

    Not a small part of the motion-picture director's work,
in addition to the preparation of the story for picture-telling
and the casting and directing of the actors, is the choice of
suitable locations for the staging of the exterior scenes and
the supervising of the studio settings, props, costumes, etc.
In these matters it seems to me that a woman is especially
well qualified to obtain the very best results, for she is dealing with subjects that are almost a second nature to her.
She takes the measure of every person, every costume, every
house, and every piece of furniture that her eye comes into
contact with, and the beauty of a stretch of landscape or a
single flower impresses her immediately. All of these things
are of the greatest value to the creator of a photodrama, and
the knowledge of them must be extensive and exact. A woman's magic touch is immediately recognized in a real home.
Is it not just as recognizable in the home of the characters
of a photoplay?

    That women make the theatre possible from the box-
office standpoint is an acknowledged fact. Theatre managers
know that their appeal must be to the woman if they would
succeed, and all of their efforts are naturally in that direction. This being the case, what a rare opportunity is offered
to women to use that inborn knowledge of just what does

appeal to them to produce photodramas that will contain that inexplicable something which is necessary to the success of every stage or screen production.

There is nothing connected with the staging of a motion picture that a woman cannot do as easily as a man, and there is no reason why she cannot completely master every technicality of the art. The technique of the drama has been mastered by so many women that it is considered as much her field as a man's and its adaptation to picture work in no way removes it from her sphere. The technique of motion-picture photography, like the technique of the drama, is fitted to a woman's activities.

It is hard for me to imagine how I could have obtained my knowledge of photography, for instance, without the months of study spent in the laboratory of the Gaumont Company in Paris at a time when motion-picture photography was in the experimental stage, and carefully continued since [in] my own laboratory in the Solax Studios in this country. It is also necessary to study stage direction by actual participation in the work, in addition to burning the midnight oil in your library, but both are as suitable, as fascinating, and as remunerative to a woman as to a man.

-- The Moving Picture World,
Vol. XXI, No. 2, July 11,
1914, p. 195.

Appendix I

THE FRENCH FILMS OF ALICE GUY:
A Filmography

compiled by Francis Lacassin

The major part of the career of Alice Guy took place during
an epoch when film directors were not credited and when the
trade press did not exist. In terms of both the number of
films and their dates, this present listing does not pretend
to be exhaustive.

The filmography is based on the list established by Alice
Guy of films which she remembered and which she gave to me
during our last interview in Brussels in 1963. These titles
are preceded by an asterisk (*). It is also based on a list
reconstituted by me from press clippings and the photograph
album which she showed to me. This second list confirms
and helps to complete the preceding one. These titles are
preceded by two asterisks (**). Finally, all the other titles
are attributed to her because no one other than Alice Guy
could have been the director.

Until the fall of 1905, when she worked in succession
with Victorin Jasset, Louis Feuillade, Etienne Arnaud, and
Romeo Bosetti, Alice Guy was Gaumont's only director. All
the production of Gaumont from that time must be attributed
to her, with the exception of actuality and documentary
shorts. However, judging by later examples, Gaumont directors were asked to utilize actuality footage for films which
were then christened, for their artistic quality, as "plein air"
or "panorama." Alice Guy was responsible for a certain number of these reels, based on footage which she shot in Spain.

All of the following titles were Gaumont productions,
filmed between 1897 and 1907. The length of each is given
in meters.

<u>April-September 1897</u>
(among others:)

1. LE PECHEUR DANS LE TORRENT. Comique et très mouve-
   menté, 16, 50 m.

2. LECON DE DANSE. Scène comique. 16,50 m.

3. BAIGNADE DANS LE TORRENT. Plein air. 16,50 m.

3a. UNE NUIT AGITEE. Scène comique, 26 m.

3b. COUCHER D'YVETTE. Three reels of 20 m. each.

4. DANSE FLEUR DE LOTUS. "A dance in the manner of
   Loie Fuller, very lively." 25 m.

4a. BALLET LIBELLA. Danse. 20 m.

5. LE PLANTON DU COLONEL. Comique. 37 m.

6. IDYLLE. "Boys and girls on a boating holiday romp in
   the grass." 22 m.

7. L'AVEUGLE. Comique. 25 m.

<u>October 1897-May 1898</u>
(among others:)

8. L'ARROSEUR ARROSE. Comique. 20 m.

9. AU REFECTOIRE. Comique. Two separate reels of 20 m.
   each.

10. EN CLASSE. Comique. Two separate reels of 16,50 m.
    each.

11. LES CAMBRIOLEURS. Comique. 22 m.

12. LE COCHER DE FIACRE ENDORMI. Comique. 27 m.

13. IDYLLE INTERROMPUE. Comique. 20 m.

14. CHEZ LE MAGNETISEUR. Comique. 20 m.

15. LES FARCES DE JOCKO. "Comic scene of transformation."
    20 m.

16. SCENE D'ESCAMOTAGE. 20 m.

17. DEMENAGEMENT A LA CLOCHE DE BOIS. 20 m.

18. JE VOUS Y PRRRRENDS! 16,50 m.

June 1898-February 1899
(among others:)

19. LECONS DE BOXE. Comique. 16,50 m.

20. LA VIE DU CHRIST. "Series of eleven novel tableaux in-
    spired by the paintings of the great masters." Total
    length: 220 m.

21. (1) LA CRECHE A BETHLEEM. 20 m.

22. (2) LA FUITE EN EGYPTE. 20 m.

23. (3) L'ENTREE A JERUSALEM. 20 m.

24. (4) LA CENE. 20 m.

25. (5) LE JARDIN DES OLIVIERS. 20 m.

26. (6) JESUS DEVANT PILATE. 20 m.

27. (7) LA FLAGELLATION. 20 m.

28. (8) LE CHEMIN DE CROIX. 20 m.

29. (9) LE CRUCIFIEMENT [sic]. 20 m.

30. (10) LA DESCENTE DE CROIX. 20 m.

31. (11) LA RESURRECTION. 20 m.

March 1899-March 1900

32. LE TONDEUR DE CHIENS. "Amusant." 20 m.

33. LE DEJEUNER DES ENFANTS. "Amusant." 20 m.

34. AU CABARET. Comique. 20 m.

35. LA MAUVAISE SOUPE. Comique. 20 m.

36. UN LUNCH. "Amusant." 20 m.

37. ERREUR JUDICIAIRE. 20 m.

38. L'AVEUGLE. 20 m.

39. LA BONNE ABSINTHE. 20 m.

40. DANSE SERPENTINE PAR MME BOB WALTER. 20 m.

41. MESAVENTURE D'UN CHARBONNIER. Comique. 20 m.

42. MONNAIE DE LAPIN. Comique. 46 m.

43. LES DANGERS DE L'ALCOOLISME. Dramatique. 30 m.

44. LE TONNELIER. Comique. 20 m.

45. TRANSFORMATIONS. Comique. 20 m.

46. LE CHIFFONNIER. Comique. 20 m.

47. RETOUR DES CHAMPS. Plein air. 20 m.

48. CHEZ LE MARECHAL-FERRANT. 20 m.

49. MARCHE A LA VOLAILLE. 20 m.

50. COURTE ECHELLE. 20 m.

51. L'ANGELUS. After the painting by Millet. 20 m.

52. BATAILLE D'OREILLERS. 20 m.

53. BATAILLE DE BOULES DE NEIGE. 20 m.

54. LE MARCHAND DE COCO. 20 m.

April–September 1900

55. AVENUE DE L'OPERA. Comique. 20 m.

56. LA PETITE MAGICIENNE. 16,50 m.

57. LECON DE DANSE. 20 m.

58. CHEZ LE PHOTOGRAPHE. 23 m.

Series: SIDNEY'S JOUJOUX

59. (1) LE BEBE. 20 m.

60. (2) L'ARLEQUINE. 16,50 m.

61. (3) LE MATELOT. 20 m.

62. (4) LE LAPIN. 20 m.

63. (5) LA PAYSANNE. 20 m.

64. (6) L'ECOSSAISE. 16,50 m.

65. (7) LA POUPEE NOIRE. 20 m.

66. (8) LE POLICHINELLE. 20 m.

67. (9) LA REINE DES JOUETS. 20 m.

68. DANS LES COULISSES. 16,50 m.

Series: AU BAL DE FLORE "Ballet Directoire of G. de Dubor.
          Music by Mlle. Jane Vieu. Danced by Mlles. Lally
          and Julyett of l'Olympia."

69. (1) VALSE DIRECTOIRE. 20 m.

70. (2) GAVOTTE DIRECTOIRE. 20 m.

71. (3) DECLARATION D'AMOUR. 20 m.

Series: BALLET JAPONAIS. "Of G. de Dubor. Music by

> Gaston Lemaire. Danced by Mlles. Barbier and Gallet of l'Opéra."

72. (1) PAS JAPONAIS. 20 m.

73. (2) PAS DE GRACE. 20 m.

74. (3) PAS DES EVENTAILS. 20 m.

75. DANSE SERPENTINE. 20 m.

76. DANSE DU PAS DES FOULARDS PAR DES ALMEES. 20 m.

77. DANCE DE L'IVRESSE. 16,50 m.

78. COUCHER D'UNE PARISIENNE. Two separate reels of 20 m. each.

Series: LES FREDAINES DE PIERETTE

79. (1) ARRIVEE DE PIERETTE ET PIERROT. 20 m.

80. (2) ARRIVEE D'ARLEQUIN. 20 m.

81. (3) SUITE DE LA DANSE. 20 m.

82. (4) DEPART D'ARLEQUIN ET DE PIERETTE. 20 m.

Series: VENUS ET ADONIS. "Ballet by M. G. De Dubor. Music by M. Mestres. Danced by Mlles. Boos and Meunier of l'Opéra."

83. (1) BADINAGE. 20 m.

84. (2) VALSE LENTE. 20 m.

85. (3) DANSE DU VOILE. 20 m.

86. (4) MORT D'ADONIS. 20 m.

87. (5) LE SANG D'ADONIS DONNANT NAISSANCE A LA ROSE ROUGE. 20 m.

88. LA TARENTELLE. 20 m.

Series: DANSE DES SAISONS

89. (1) LE PRINTEMPS: DANSE DES ROSES. 20 m.

90. (2) L'ETE: DANSE DE LA MOISSON. 20 m.

91. (3) L'AUTOMNE: DANSE DES VENDAGES.

92. (4) L'HIVER: DANSE DE LA NEIGE. 20 m.

93. *LA SOURCE. "Naughty." 60 m.

94. DANSE DU PAPILLON. Two reels of 20 m. each.

95. *LA FEE AUX CHOUX, OU LA NAISSANCE DES ENFANTS.
    "A fairy takes up the living babies which she gathers
    from cabbages. A very great success." Actress:
    Yvonne Mugnier-Serand. 20 m. (Alice Guy claims
    this as her first film, produced in 1896. However,
    it appears as No. 379 in the Gaumont catalog and
    might be dated between August and September 1900.
    No. 397 in the catalog is an actuality reel recording
    a mayors' meeting and banquet presided over by
    French President Loubet, which took place, according
    to contemporary press reports, on September 22, 1900.
    Alice Guy, betrayed by her memory, is in contradic-
    tion of herself in affirming that she inaugurated the
    production of fictional films at Gaumont. Either she
    did not, which is highly improbable, or else she did
    and La Fée aux choux is not her first film.)†

96. LA CONCIERGE. Comique. 20 m.

October-November 1900

Series: DANSES. "by Mlle Valentine Brouat, a dancer of
        whom the press has written eloquently and who made
        her debut in Paris in October 1900."

---

†Simone Blaché vehemently disagrees with Francis Lacassin.
She is positive that La Fée aux choux was her mother's first
film, and that it was produced in 1896. She maintains that
the numbers adopted in the Gaumont catalog are irrelevant.

97. (1) L'HABANERA. 20 m.

98. (2) PAS DU POIGNARD. 20 m.

99. (3) PAS DE L'EVENTAIL. 20 m.

100. CHIRURGIE FIN DE SIECLE. Comique a trucs. Two
     reels of 20 m. each.

101. UND RAGE DE DENTS. Comique a trucs. 20 m.

102. SAUT HUMIDIFIE DE M. PLICK. Acted by the clowns
     Plick and Plock. 20 m.

Winter 1900-1901

103. LA DANSE DU VENTRE. "Three bohemians in an Al-
     gerian danse." 20 m.

104. LAVATORY MODERNE. 16,50 m.

105. LECTURE QUOTIDIENNE. "Transformation scene." 20 m.

May-June 1901

Series: FOLIES MASQUEES. "Fantasy by MM. Henry Darges
     and René Louis. Music by Mlle. Jane Vieu. As
     presented at l'Olympia. Actors: Mlle. Barbage
     (Pierrot), Mlle Renée Dudley (Pierette), Mlle. Lally
     (Colombine), and Mlles. Reine and Bonheur (traves-
     tis).

106. (1) SCENE D'AMOUR. 35 m.

107. (2) PAS DE COLOMBINE. 30 m.

108. (3) SCENE D'IVRESSE. 35 m.

109. FRIVOLITE. "Divertissement-pantomime by Mlle. Jane
     Vieu." Actress: Mlle. Julie Souplet of l'Opéra (la
     grisette). 60 m.

July 1901

110. LES VAGUES. "Divertissement-pantomime by Mlle. Jane Vieu." Acted by Mlles. Juliette Souplet and Geneviève Koch of l'Opéra. 32 m.

111. DANSES BASQUES. "Divertissement-pantomime by Mlle. Jane Vieu." Acted by Mlles. Juliette Souplet and Geneviève Koch. 32 m.

1901

112. HUSSARDS ET GRISETTES.

113. CHARMANT FROUFROU.

114. TEL EST PRIS QUI CROYAIT PRENDRE.

April 1902

115. LA FIOLE ENCHANTEE. 16,50 m.

116. L'EQUILIBRISTE. 20 m.

May-September 1902

117. EN FACTION. Comique. 30 m.

118. LA PREMIERE GAMELLE. Comique. 30 m.

119. LA DENT RECALCITRANTE. Comique. 25 m.

120. LE MARCHAND DE BALLONS. Comique. 25 m.

121. LES CHIENS SAVANTS. Excellent views. Actress: Miss Dundee. 120 m.

Series: MISS LINA ESBRARD DANSEUSE COSMOPOLITE ET SERPENTINE

122. (1) DANSE FANTAISISTE. 20 m.

123. (2) DANS SERPENTINE.   25 m.

124. (3) DANSE EXCENTRIQUE.   20 m.

125. (4) LA GIGUE.   "Recommended for phonograph accompaniment."   25 m.

October 1902

126. LES CLOWNS "Very comic reel."   80 m.

127. *SAGE-FEMME DE PREMIERE CLASSE.   "Very great success."   (This was an enlarged version of LA FEE AUX CHOUX.)   100 m.

128. QUADRILLE REALISTE.   40 m.

129. UND SCENE EN CABINET PARTICULIER VUE A TRAVERS LE TROU DE LA SERRURE.   "Very fine and funny reel."

130. FARCES DE CUISINIERE.   Comic.   55 m.

131. DANSE MAURESQUE.   Actress: Mlle Barami.   30 m.

132. LE LION SAVANT.   Comic.   41 m.

November 1902

133. LE POMMIER.   "Country scene."   30 m.

134. LA COUR DES MIRACLES.   "Original, comic and very interesting."   52 m.

135. LA GAVOTTE.   Dance.   52 m.

136. TROMPE MAIS CONTENT.   "Comic and unusual."   75 m.

1902

137. FRUITS DE SAISON

138. POUR SECOUER LA SALADE

February 1903

139. POTAGE INDIGESTE. Comic. 20 m.

140. ILLUSIONNISTE RENVERSANT. 25 m.

March 1903

141. LE FIANCE ENSORCELE. "Comic scene with transformation." 50 m.

142. LES APACHES PAS VEINARDS. 20 m.

143. LES AVENTURES D'UN VOYAGEUR TROP PRESSE.
"Comic scene of transformation." 50 m.

April 1903

144. NE BOUGEONS PLUS. Comedy with tricks. 20 m.

145. COMMENT MONSIEUR PREND SON BAIN. Comic: 40 m.

146. LA MAIN DU PROFESSEUR HAMILTON OU LE ROI DES
DOLLARS. 25 m.

May 1903

147. SERVICE PRECIPITE. Comic. 25 m.

148. LA POULE FANTAISISTE. Scene with tricks. 30 m.

June-July 1903

149. MODELAGE EXPRESS. 37 m.

150. FAUST ET MEPHISTOPHELES" Fairytale. 44 m.

151. LUTTEURS AMERICAINS. Comedy with tricks. 20 m.

152. LA VALISE ENCHANTEE. Comedy with tricks. 34 m.

153. COMPAGNONS DE VOYAGE ENCOMBRANTS. Comedy
     with tricks. 30 m.

154. *CAKE-WALK DE LA PENDULE. Comedy with tricks.
     40 m.

155. REPETITION DANS UN CIRQUE. 40 m.

156. JOCKO MUSICIEN. Comic. Actor: the monkey, Jocko.
     40 m.

September-October 1903

157. LES BRACONNIERS. Drama 67 m.

158. *LA LIQUEUR DU COUVENT. Comic. 40 m.

November 1903

159. LE VOLEUR SACRILEGE. 30 m.

160. ENLEVEMENT EN AUTOMOBILE ET MARIAGE PRECIPITE.
     "Recommended." 90 m.

December 1903-March 1904

161. SECOURS AUX NAUFRAGES. Drama. 200 m.

162. LA MOUCHE. Comic. 24 m.

163. LA CHASSE AU CAMBRIOLEUR. Drama. 50 m.

164. NOS BONS ETUDIANTS. Comic. 30 m.

165. LES SURPRISES DE L'AFFICHAGE. Comic. 34 m.

166. COMME ON FAIT SON LIT ON SE COUCHE. Comedy with
     tricks. 64 m.

167. LE POMPON MALENCONTREUX. Comic. 21 m.

168. COMMENT ON DISPERSE LES FOULES. Comic. 38 m.

169. LES ENFANTS DU MIRACLE. 47 m.

170. PIERROT ASSASSIN. Fairytale. 80 m.

171. LES DEUX RIVAUX. "Recommended" comedy. 76 m.

April 1904

172. *L'ASSASSINAT DU COURRIER DE LYON. Drama. 122
     m.

Series: VIEILLES ESTAMPES. Total length: 80 m.

173. (1) LA LECON DE PIPEAU.

174. (2) L'OISEAU ENVOLE.

175. (3) LA GAVOTTE DE LA REINE.

176. (4) APRES LA FETE.

177. MAUVAIS COEUR PUNI. Dramatic comedy. 50 m.

178. MAGIE NOIRE. Scene with tricks. 60 m.

179. RAFLE DE CHIENS. Comic. 16,50 m.

180. CAMBRIOLEUR ET AGENT. Dramatic comedy. 35 m.

Series: SCENES DIRECTOIRE. Total length: 92 m.

181. (1) LA PARTIE DE COLIN-MAILLARD.

182. (2) RIVALITE.

183. (3) LA CHARMILLE.

184. DUEL TRAGIQUE. Dramatic Comedy. 35 m.

185. L'ATTAQUE D'UNE DILIGENCE. 125 m.

May 1904

186. CULTURE INTENSIVE OU LE VIEUX MARI. Comic. 37 m.

187. CIBLE HUMAINE. "Very comic." 30 m.

188. TRANSFORMATIONS. 22 m.

189. LE JOUR DU TERME. 95 m.

June 1904

190. ROBERT MACAIRE ET BERTRAND. Comic. 14 m.

191. ELECTROCUTEE. Comic. 27 m.

192. LE REVE DU CHASSEUR. Comedy with tricks. 30 m.

August 1904

193. LE MONOLUTTEUR. Comic. 23 m.

194. LES PETITS COUPEURS DE BOIS VERT. "Recommended" drama. (claimed by Alice Guy under the title: LES PETITS VOLEURS DE BOIS VERT). 80 m.

195. CLOWN EN SAC. Comic. 43 m.

196. *TRISTE FIN D'UN VIEUX SAVANT. Comic. 50 m.

197. LE TESTAMENT DE PIERROT. Fairytale. 70 m.

198. LES SECRETS DE LA PRESTIDIGITATION DEVOILES. Comic with tricks. 69 m.

199. LA FAIM... L'OCCASION... L'HERBE TENDRE... Comic. 70 m.

200. *MILITAIRE ET NOURRICE. Comic. 45 m.

201. *LA PREMIERE CIGARETTE. "Highly recommended." 60 m.

202. DEPART POUR LES VACANCES. "Very comic." 110 m.

203. TENTATIVE D'ASSASSINAT EN CHEMIN DE FER. Drama.
     60 m.

September 1904

204. PARIS LA NUIT OU EXPLOITS D'APACHES A MONT-
     MARTRE. 95 m.

205. *CONCOURS DE BEBES. "Comic scene for any showing."
     45 m.

206. ERREUR DE POIVROT. Comic. 23 m.

October 1904

207. *VOLEE PAR LES BOHEMIENS. Drama. "Recommended."
     Alternate title: RAPT D'ENFANT PAR LES ROMAN-
     ICHELS. 225 m.

208. LES BIENFAITS DU CINEMATOGRAPHE. Comic. 40 m.

209. PATISSIER ET RAMONEUR. Comic. 34 m.

210. GAGE D'AMOUR. Comic. 33 m.

November 1904

211. *L'ASSASSINAT DE LA RUE DU TEMPLE. Drama in 8
     scenes. Alternate title: LE CRIME DE LA RUE DU
     TEMPLE. 200 m.

212. LE REVEIL DU JARDINIER. "Highly recommended comic
     scene." 28 m.

213. LES CAMBRIOLEURS DE PARIS. Drama. 83 m.

December 1904-May 1905

(During this period the only fiction films
circulated were produced by Gaumont-British.)

June 1905

214. REHABILITATION. Great dramatic scene. 250 m.

July 1905

215. *DOUANIERS ET CONTREBANDIERS. Comic. Alternate
title: LA GUERITE. 79 m.

216. LE BEBE EMBARRASSANT. "Very funny." 133 m.

August 1905

217. COMMENT ON DORT A PARIS! 91 m.

September 1905

218. LE LORGNON ACCUSATEUR. Comic. 20 m.

219. LA CHARITE DU PRESTIDIGITATEUR. Comedy with
tricks. 65 m.

October 1905

220. *UNE NOCE AU LAC SAINT-FARGEAU. Comic. Claimed
by Alice Guy under the title: MARIEE DU LAC
SAINT-FARGEAU. 137 m.

221. LE KEPI. 49 m.

222. *LE PANTALON COUPE. Comic. 80 m.

223. *LE PLATEAU. 50 m.

224. ROMEO PRIS AU PIEGE. 58 m.

225. CHIEN JOUANT A LA BALLE. 25 m.

226. LE FANTASSIN GUIGNARD. 96 m.

227. LA STATUE. Comic. 120 m.

228. VILLA DEVALISEE. Comic. 80 m.

November 1905

229. MORT DE ROBERT MACAIRE ET BERTRAND. Dramatic
     comedy. 163 m.

230. LE PAVE. Comic. 23 m.

231. *LES MACONS. "Very comic scene." Actors: the
     O'Mers.

December 1905

232. *LA ESMERALDA. 290 m.

233. PEINTRE ET IVROGNE. Comic. 20 m.

234. ON EST PIOVROT, MAIS ON A DU COEUR. Comic. 80 m.

235. AU POULAILLER! 20 m.

January 1906

236. *LA FEE PRINTEMPS. "Very graceful scene." 32 m.

237. LA VIE DU MARIN. 160 m.

238. LA CHAUSSETTE. Comic. 36 m.

239. *LA MESSE DE MINUIT. "Christmas story." 127 m.

240. PAUVRE POMPIER. Comic. 107 m.

February 1906

241. LE REGIMENT MODERNE. Comic. 142 m.

242. *LES DRUIDES. Drama. 36 m.

Series: VOYAGE EN ESPAGNE. Documentary

243. (1) LE MONASTERE DE MONTSERRAT. 16 m.

244. (2) MADRID. PLACE CASTELLAR; MINISTERE DE LA
GUERRE; JARDIN DU PRADO. 72 m.

245. (3) MADRID. CALLE DE SEVILLA; PUERTA DEL SOL;
PALACIO REAL; PLAZA DE TOROS. 90 m.

246. (4) MADRID, PANORAMA DE LAS VENTAS. 56 m.

247. (5) MADRID. FONTAINE DE LAS VENTAS. 44 m.

248. (6) CORDOUE. FONTAINE ET PATIO DE LAS NARAN-
JAS; MOSQUEE. Panorama. 64 m.

249. (7) SEVILLE. JARDINS ET INTERIEURS DE L'ALCAZAR.
51 m.

250. (8) SEVILLE. PANORAMA DU PORT; LA CATHEDRALE;
LA TOUR DE L'OR. 27 m.

251. (9) GRENADE. L'ALHAMBRA (Court of the Lions.) 31 m.

252. (10) GRENADE. Panorama. 50 m.

253. (11) DANSES GITANES. MARENGARO. 49 m.

254. (12) DANSES GITANES. SEVILLANE. 47 m.

255. (13) DANSES GITANES. 42 m.

256. (14) DANSES GITANES. 63 m.

257. (15) ALGESIRAS. Panorama. 50 m.

March 1906

*LA VIE DU CHRIST. Twenty-five tableaux (after the illus-
trations of James Tissot). Total length: 600 m.

258. (1) ARRIVEE A BETHLEEM. 41 m.

259. (2) LA NATIVITE. 43 m.

260. (3) LE SOMMEIL DE JESUS. 30 m.

261. (4) LA SAMARITAINE. 18 m.

262. (5) MIRACLE DE LA FILLE DE JAIRE. 30 m.

263. (6) MARIE MAGDELEINE. 22 m.

264. (7) LES RAMEAUX. 16 m.

265. (8) LA CENE. 26 m.

266. (9) AU JARDIN DES OLIVIERS. 20 m.

267. (10) LA VEILLEE. 12 m.

268. (11) LA TRAHISON ET L'ARRESTATION. 22 m.

269. (12) JESUS DEVANT CAIPHE. 41 m.

270. (13) LE RENIEMENT DE SAINT PIERRE. 32 m.

271. (14) JESUS DEVANT PILATE. 30 m.

272. (15) LA FLAGELLATION. 32 m.

273. (16) ECCE HOMO. 18 m.

274. (17) CHARGEMENT DE LA CROIX. 15 m.

275. (18) JESUS TOMBE POUR LA PREMIERE FOIS. 31 m.

276. (19) SAINTE VERONIQUE. 25 m.

277. (20) LA MONTEE EN GOLGOTHA. 40 m.

278. (21) LA CRUCIFIXION. 23 m.

279. (22) L'AGONIE. 16 m.

280. (23) DESCENTE DE CROIX. 30 m.

281. (24) LA MISE AU TOMBEAU. 15 m.

282. (25) LA RESURRECTION. 31 m.

April-August 1906

283. *CONSCIENCE DE PRETRE. "Highly recommended drama-
     tic scene." 150 m.

284. *L'HONNEUR DU CORSE. Drama. 107 m. Alternate
     title: LA VENDETTA.

285. *J'AI UN HANNETON DANS MON PANTALON. Comic.
     68 m.

286. *LE FILS DU GARDE-CHASSE. Drama. 83 m.

287. *COURSE DE TAUREAUX A NIMES. "Beautiful move-
     ments of the toreador Machaquito." Cameraman:
     Herbert Blaché. 161 m.

288. *LA PEGRE DE PARIS. Drama. 260 m.

September 1906

289. *LEVRES CLOSES. Drama. (Remade in the U.S.A.
     under the title: SEALED LIPS.) 77 m.

October 1906

290. *LA CRINOLINE. Comic. 37 m.

291. *LA VOITURE CELLULAIRE. Comic. (Played by the
     celebrated troupe of the O'Mers) 37 m.

November-December 1906

292. *LA MARATRE. "Recommended dramatic scene." 175 m.

293. *LE MATELAS ALCOOLIQUE. Comic. 218 m.

294. *A LA RECHERCHE D'UN APPARTEMENT. Comic.
     120 m.

1907

295. *LA VERITE SUR L'HOMME-SINGE. Comic. 160 m.
     Alternate title: BALLET DE SINGE.

May 1907

296. *DEMENAGEMENT A LA CLOCHE DE BOIS. Comic. Ac-
     tors: The O'Mers. Remake of the 20 m. reel of the
     same title in 1898. 149 m.

1907

297. *LES GENDARMES. Comic. 104 m.

298. *SUR LA BARRICADE. Drama. Alternate title: L'EN-
     FANT DE LA BARRICADE. 88 m.

On the list established for me by Alice Guy in 1963 appear
several titles which I have been unable to find:

   LUI

   L'ASILE DE NUIT

   LE PARALYTIQUE

   PROFESSEUR DE LANGUES VIVANTES

   LA FEVE ENCHANTEE

   LA LEGENDE DE SAINT NICOLAS

   LE NOEL DE PIERROT

She also cites in her autogiography some other equally elusive
titles:

   LA MOMIE

   LILLIPUT ET GULLIVER

   L'OGRE ET LE PETIT POUCET

AU TELEPHONE

AMOUREUX ARAMIS

UNE NOCE A ROBINSON (acted by the O'Mers)

Some of these may have been working titles. Others may
have been unreleased for technical reasons. For example,
Alice Guy confirmed that <u>Mireille</u>, filmed in the Camargue with
Louis Feuillade, proved unusable after the negative had been
developed. It was stripped by what technicians of the period
called "effluves."

Phonoscenes Gaumont, 1900-1907

These are "talking films," with the sound recorded on wax
cylinders. They were limited to songs, dances, and mono-
logues. Alice Guy directed the following, among others, and
without precise release dates but in chronological order:

*Series: CARMEN (Opera in French)

299. (1) DUO DU II ACTE. JE VAIS DANSER. 63 m.

300. (2) LA FLEUR QUE TU M'AVAIS JETEE. 60 m.

301. (3) NON, TU NE M'AIMES PAS. 63 m.

302. (4) AIR DES CARTES. 56 m.

*Series: MIREILLE (Opera in French)

303. (1) O MAGALI. 57 m.

304. (2) ANGES DU PARADIS. 60 m.

305. (3) TRAHIR VINCENT. 59 m.

306. (4) HEUREUX PETIT BERGER. 43 m.

307. (5) VALSE. 39 m.

*Series: CARMEN (suite)

308. (5) MA MERE, JE LA VOIS. 70 m.

309. (6) HABANERAS. 57 m.

310. (7) PRES DES REMPARTS. 36 m.

311. (8) LES TRINGLES. 58 m.

312. (9) [unidentified title]

313. (10) LE DUEL. 59 m.

314. (11) DUO DU IVe ACTE, 1re PARTIE. 60 m.

315. (12) LA MORT. (IVe acte, 2e partie). 70 m.

*Series: LES DRAGONS DE VILLARS (Opera in French)

316. (1) NE PARLE PAS. 55 m.

317. (2) COUPLETS DE L'ERMITE. 53 m.

318. (3) QUAND LE DRAGON. 55 m.

319. (4) EH BIEN! SYLVAIN. 55 m.

320. (5) CHANSON PROVENCALE. 61 m.

321. (6) LE SAGE QUI S'EVEILLE. 53 m.

322. (7) ESPOIR CHARMANT. 69 m.

323. (8) DUO "MOI, JOLIE". 66 m.

324. (9) AIR DES MULES. 66 m.

*Series: MIGNON (Opera in French)

325. (1) LEGERES HIRONDELLES. 56 m.

326. (2) STYRIENNES. 59 m.

327. (3) ADIEU, MIGNON. 44 m.

328. (4) JE SUIS TITANIA. 60 m.

329. (5) AS-TU SOUFFERT? 66 m.

330. (6) ELLE NE CROYAIT PAS. 68 m.

331. (7) BERCEUSE. 61 m.

*Series: FAUST (Opera in French)

332. (1) SALUT, O MON DERNIER MATIN. 72 m.

333. (2) DUO DU Ier ACTE, Ire partie. 70 m.

334. (3) DUO DU Ier ACTE, 2e partie. 65 m.

335. (4) DUO DU Ier ACTE, 3e partie. 42 m.

336. (5) FAITES-LUI MES AVEUX. 56 m.

337. (6) DEMEURE CHASTE ET PURE. 69 m.

338. (7) LA COUPE DU ROI DE THULE. 64 m.

339. (8) AIR DES BIJOUX. 75 m.

340. (9) QUATUOR DU JARDIN. 62 m.

341. (10) EVOCATION. 34 m.

342. (11) LAISSE-MOI CONTEMPLER TON VISAGE. 57 m.

343. (12) O NUIT D'AMOUR. 60 m.

344. (13) IL M'AIME. 47 m.

345. (14) DIVINE PURETE. 40 m.

346. (15) SCENE DE L'EGLISE, 1re partie. 58 m.

347. (16) SCENE DE L'EGLISE, 2e partie. 78 m.

348. (17) LA SERENADE. 61 m.

349. (18) TRIO DU DUEL, 1re partie. 34 m.

350. (19) TRIO DU DUEL, 2e partie. 44 m.

351. (20) LA PRISON. LE JOUR VA LUIRE. 65 m.

352. (21) LA PRISON. MON COEUR EST PENETRE. 60 m.

353. (22) LA PRISON. Trio final. 62 m.

*Series: POLIN

354. (1) LE PORTAIT DE LEDA. Monologue. 52 m.

355. (2) LE GOSSE DU COMMANDANT. Monologue. 62 m.

356. (3) LA BALANCE AUTOMATIQUE. Comic song. 57 m.

357. (4) LA VENUS DU LUXEMBOURG. Idem. 50 m.

358. (5) LES QUESTIONS DE LOUISE. Idem. 47 m.

359. (6) LE FROTTEUR DE LA COLONELLE. Idem. 44 m.

360. (7) L'AUTO DU COLON. Idem. 39 m.

361. (8) L'ANATOMIE DU CONSCRIT. Idem. 50 m.

362. (9) LE PEPIN DE LA DAME. Idem. 47 m.

363. (10) SITUATION INTERESSANTE. Monologue. 59 m.

364. (11) CHEZ LES LUTTEURS. Comic song. 48 m.

365. (12) LA BELLE CUISINIERE. Comic song. e. 52 m.

366. (13) LA LECTURE DU RAPPORT. Monologue. 76 m.

*Series: MAYOL

367. (1) LA FIFILLE A SA MEMERE. Comic song. 48 m.

368. (2) LE PETIT PANIER. Idem. 54 m.

369. (3) LE PETIT GREGOIRE. Idem. 54 m.

370. (4) VIENS, POUPOULE. Idem. 53 m.

371. (5) LILAS BLANC. Sad song. 63 m.

372. (6) JEUNE HOMME ET TROTTIN. Comic song. 62 m.

373. (7) LA POLKA DES TROTTINS. Idem. 52 m.

374. (8) LA PAIMPOLAISE. Breton song in French. 56 m.

375. (9) C'EST UNE INGENUE. Comic song. 56 m.

376. (10) SI CA T'VA. Idem. 51 m.

377. (11) A LA CABANE BAMBOU. Idem. 53 m.

378. (12) QUESTIONS INDISCRETES. Idem. 56 m.

379. (13) LA MATTCHICHE. Idem. 50 m.

*Series: DRANEM (Comic songs)

380. (1) ALLUMEUR-MARCHE. 45 m.

381. (2) LE TROU DE MON QUAI. 49 m.

382. (3) VALSONS. 46 m.

383. (4) V'LA LE RETAMEUR. 51 m.

384. (5) LES P'TITS POIS. 41 m.

385. (6) L'ENFANT DU CORDONNIER. 45 m.

386. (7) ETRE LEGUME. 38 m.

387. (8) LE CUCURBITACEE. 44 m.

388. (9) LE BOLERO COSMOPOLITE. 49 m.

389. (10) BONSOIR, M'SIEURS, DAMES. 47 m.

390. (11) LE VRAI JIU-JITSU. 48 m.

391. (12) FIVE O'CLOCK TEA. 57 m.

*Series recorded in Spain:

392. (1) LA GATITA BLANCA MACHICHA. 49 m.

393. (2) LA GATITA BLANCA. Couplet n° 2. 46 m.

394. (3) EL HUSAR DE LA GUARDIA. Duo. 55 m.

395. (4) GIGANTES Y CABEZUDOS. 64 m.

396. (5) LA VIEJECITA. 60 m.

397. (6) EL AMIGO DEL ALMA. 60 m.

398. (7) EL ARTE DE SER BONITA. 45 m.

399. (8) LAS CARCELERAS. 69 m.

400. (9) LA TEMPESTAD. 60 m.

401. (10) EL HUSAR DE LA GUARDIA, n° 2. 63 m.

402. (11) EL CORO FREGIO. 81 m.

403. LA PRIERE DE GOUNOD. 69 m.

The list which Alice Guy gave to me in 1963 also included the following titles, which cannot be found:

LES CLOCHES DE CORVEVILLE

MADAME ANGOT

LA VIVANDIERE

LE COUTEAU (acted by Theodore Botrel)

Appendix J

THE AMERICAN FILMS OF
ALICE GUY BLACHE:
A Filmography

compiled by Anthony Slide

The first 331 films on this list were produced by the Solax
Company. All are one reel in length unless otherwise indicated. The release date is given immediately following the
title. Obviously Alice Guy Blaché did not direct all of the
Solax films, but she was involved in the production of them
all as the equivalent of supervising director and producer.
There is no record as to who directed those films which Madame Blaché did not personally direct, but several of them
would appear to be the work of Edward Warren.

Unless otherwise indicated, all films from No. 332 on-
ward were directed by Alice Guy Blaché.

1. A CHILD'S SACRIFICE. October 21, 1910.

2. THE SERGEANT'S DAUGHTER. October 28, 1910.

3. A FATEFUL GIFT. November 4, 1910.

4. A WIDOW AND HER CHILD. November 11, 1910.

5. HER FATHER'S SIN. November 18, 1910.

6. ONE TOUCH OF NATURE. November 25, 1910.

7. WHAT IS TO BE, WILL BE. December 2, 1910.

8. LADY BETTY'S STRATEGY. December 9, 1910.

9. TWO SUITS. December 16, 1910.

10. THE PAWNSHOP. December 23, 1910.

11. MRS. RICHARD DARE. December 30, 1910.

12. THE NIGHTCAP. January 6, 1911.

13. SALMON FISHING IN CANADA. January 6, 1911.

14. THE GIRL AND THE BURGLAR. January 13, 1911.

15. A REPORTER'S ROMANCE. January 20, 1911.

16. HIS BEST FRIEND. January 27, 1911.

17. RING OF LOVE. February 3, 1911.

18. MIXED PETS. February 10, 1911.

19. CORINNE IN DOLLYLAND. February 17, 1911.

20. LOVE'S TEST. February 24, 1911.

21. A COSTLY PLEDGE. March 3, 1911.

22. OUT OF THE ARCTIC. March 8, 1911.

23. PUT OUT. March 10, 1911.

24. CARIBOU HUNTING. March 10, 1911.

25. A MIDNIGHT VISITOR. March 15, 1911.

26. HIGHLANDS OF NEW BRUNSWICK, CANADA. March 15,
     1911.

27. A HINDU PRINCE. March 17, 1911.

28. CUPID'S VICTORY. March 22, 1911.

29. OUT OF THE DEPTHS. March 24, 1911.

30. A PACKAGE OF TROUBLE. March 29, 1911.

31. SHE WAS NOT AFRAID. March 29, 1911.

32. THE MILL OF THE GODS. March 31, 1911.

33. A MAID'S REVENGE. April 5, 1911.

34. THE ROSE OF THE CIRCUS. April 7, 1911.

35. TRAMP STRATEGY. April 12, 1911.

36. THE SCHEME THAT FAILED. April 12, 1911.

37. THE LITTLE FLOWER GIRL. April 14, 1911.

38. THE OLD EXCUSE. April 19, 1911.

39. THE VOICE OF HIS CONSCIENCE. April 21, 1911.

40. THE COUNT OF NO ACCOUNT. April 26, 1911.

41. ACROSS THE MEXICAN LINE. April 28, 1911.

42. SENSIBLE DAD. May 3, 1911.

43. THE SOMNAMBULIST. May 5, 1911.

44. NEARLY A HERO. May 10, 1911.

45. BENEATH THE MOON. May 10, 1911.

46. BETWEEN LIFE AND DUTY. May 12, 1911.

47. HIS DUMB WIFE. May 17, 1911.

48. IN THE NICK OF TIME. May 19, 1911.

49. THE DEVIL IN A TIN CUP. May 24, 1911.

50. AN OFFICER AND A GENTLEMAN. May 26, 1911.

51. A MARVELOUS COW. May 31, 1911.

52. NEVER TOO LATE TO MEND. June 2, 1911.

53. BRIDGET THE FLIRT. June 7, 1911.

54. A MEXICAN GIRL'S LOVE. June 9, 1911.

55. A BAD EGG. June 14, 1911.

56. A DAUGHTER OF THE NAVAJO. June 16, 1911.

57. CUPID AND THE COMET. June 21, 1911.

58. JOHNNIE WATERS THE GARDEN. June 21, 1911.

59. MARKED FOR LIFE. June 23, 1911.

60. THE FASCINATING WIDOW. June 28, 1911.

61. A TERRIBLE CATASTROPHE. June 28, 1911.

62. GREATER LOVE HATH NO MAN. June 30, 1911.

63. STARTING SOMETHING. July 5, 1911.

64. THE SILENT SIGNAL. July 7, 1911.

65. BABY'S RATTLE. July 12, 1911.

66. THAT JUNE BUG. July 12, 1911.

67. THE GIRL AND THE BRONCHO BUSTER. July 14, 1911.

68. ALL ABOARD FOR RENO. July 19, 1911.

69. SERGEANT DILLON'S BRAVERY. July 21, 1911.

70. THE DOUBLE ELOPEMENT. July 26, 1911.

71. OUTWITTED BY HORSE AND LARIAT. July 28, 1911.

72. WHEN REUBEN CAME TO TOWN. August 2, 1911.

73. THE MASCOT OF TROOP "C" August 4, 1911.

74. HIS WIFE'S INSURANCE. August 9, 1911.

75. A BUM AND A BOMB. August 9, 1911.

76. AN ENLISTED MAN'S HONOR. August 11, 1911.

77. THE PHONEY RING. August 16, 1911.

78. LET NO MAN PUT ASUNDER. August 18, 1911.

79. A GAY BACHELOR. August 23, 1911.

80. THE STAMPEDE. August 25, 1911.

81. THE PATCHED SHOE. August 30, 1911.

82. THE HOLD-UP. September 1, 1911.

83. HECTOR'S INHERITANCE. September 6, 1911.

84. THE BEST POLICY. September 8, 1911.

85. HER UNCLE'S WILL. September 13, 1911.

86. THE ALTERED MESSAGE. September 15, 1911.

87. OH! YOU STENOGRAPHER! September 20, 1911.

88. NELLIE'S SOLDIER. September 22, 1911.

89. HOW HOPKINS RAISED THE RENT. September 27, 1911.

90. AN ITALIAN'S GRATITUDE. September 29, 1911.

91. A BREEZY MORNING. October 4, 1911.

92. HIS SISTER'S SWEETHEART. October 6, 1911.

93. HE WAS A MILLIONAIRE. October 11, 1911.

94. HIS MOTHER'S HYMN. October 13, 1911.

95. A CORNER IN CRIMINALS. October 18, 1911.

96. A LOVER'S RUSE. October 18, 1911.

97. HIS BETTER SELF. October 20, 1911.

98. PERCY AND HIS SQUAW. October 25, 1911.

99. FOR BIG BROTHER'S SAKE. October 27, 1911.

100. FOLLOWING COUSIN'S FOOTSTEPS. November 1, 1911.

101. A HEROINE OF THE REVOLUTION. November 3, 1911.

102. AN INTERRUPTED ELOPEMENT. November 8, 1911.

103. GRANDMOTHER LOVE. November 10, 1911.

104. BABY NEEDS MEDICINE. November 15, 1911.

105. ONLY A SQUAW. November 17, 1911.

106. HUSBANDS WANTED. November 22, 1911.

107. THE WILL OF PROVIDENCE. November 24, 1911.

108. A TROUBLESOME PICTURE. November 29, 1911.

109. LIFE ON BOARD A BATTLESHIP. November 29, 1911.

110. A REVOLUTIONARY ROMANCE. December 1, 1911.

111. BABY'S CHOICE. December 6, 1911.

112. THE PAPER MAKING INDUSTRY. December 6, 1911.

113. THE LITTLE SHOE. December 8, 1911.

114. FICKLE BRIDGET. December 13, 1911.

115. THE LITTLE KIDDIE MINE. December 15, 1911.

116. LOVE, WHISKERS, AND LETTERS. December 20, 1911.

117. THE VIOLIN MAKER OF NUREMBERG. December 22, 1911.

118. WHEN MARIAN WAS MARRIED. December 27, 1911.

119. THE DIVIDED RING. December 29, 1911.

120. CHRISTMAS PRESENTS. December 31, 1911.

121. HIS MUSICAL SOUL. January 3, 1911.

122. OUR POOR RELATION. January 5, 1912.

123. ECONOMICAL BROWN. January 10, 1912.

124. BLACK SHEEP. January 12, 1912.

125. BY THE HAND OF A CHILD. January 14, 1912.

126. PARSON SUE. January 17, 1912.

127. A MAN'S MAN. January 19, 1912.

128. THE LEGEND OF THE BALANCED ROCK. January 21, 1912.

129. THE LITTLE SOLDIER. January 24, 1912.

130. MEMORIES OF '49. January 26, 1912.

131. FROZEN ON LOVE'S TRAIL. January 28, 1912.

132. THE WONDERFUL OSWEGO FALLS. January 31, 1912.

133. THE FIXER FIXED. January 31, 1912.

134. MIGNON. February 2, 1912.

135. THE SNOWMAN. February 4, 1912.

136. A GUILTY CONSCIENCE. February 7, 1912.

137. MRS. CRANSTON'S JEWELS. February 9, 1912.

138. LEND ME YOUR WIFE. February 11, 1912.

139. BESSIE'S SUITORS. February 14, 1912.

140. A TERRIBLE LESSON. February 16, 1912.

141. THE WISE WITCH OF FAIRYLAND. February 18, 1912.

142. HUBBY DOES THE WASHING. February 21, 1912.

143. GOD DISPOSES. February 23, 1912.

144. HIS LORDSHIP'S WHITE FEATHER. February 25, 1912.

145. ALGIE THE MINER. February 28, 1912.

146. BLIGHTED LIVES. March 1, 1912.

147. SEALED LIPS. March 6, 1912.

148. THE ANIMATED BATHTUB. March 8, 1912.

149. THE BOARDING HOUSE HEIRESS. March 13, 1912.

150. FALLING LEAVES. March 15, 1912.

151. COUNT HENRI, THE HUNTER. March 20, 1912.

152. THE BACHELOR'S CLUB. March 20, 1912.

153. THE CHILD OF THE TENEMENTS. March 22, 1912.

154. BILLY'S SHOES. March 27, 1912.

155. HANDLE WITH CARE. March 29, 1912.

156. THE WITCH'S NECKLACE. April 3, 1912.

157. BILLY'S TROUBLESOME GRIP. April 5, 1912.

158. THE DETECTIVE'S DOG. April 10, 1912.

159. BILLY'S NURSE. April 12, 1912.

160. SAVED BY A CAT. April 17, 1912.

161. BILLY, THE DETECTIVE. April 10, 1912.

162. THE SEWER. April 24, 1912.

163. BILLY'S INSOMNIA. April 26, 1912.

164. THE REFORMATION OF MARY. May 1, 1912.

165. A QUESTION OF HAIR. May 3, 1912.

166. THE WOOING OF ALICE. May 8, 1912.

167. AUTO SUGGESTION. May 10, 1912.

168. SOULS IN THE SHADOW. May 15, 1912.

169. IN THE YEAR 2000. May 17, 1912.

170. THE GLORY OF LIGHT. May 22, 1912.

171. THE KNIGHT IN ARMOR. May 24, 1912.

172. A MESSAGE FROM BEYOND. May 29, 1912.

173. JUST A BOY. May 31, 1912.

174. THE OLD VIOLIN. June 5, 1912.

175. THE DOG-GONE QUESTION. June 7, 1912.

176. BILLY BOY. June 7, 1912.

177. MICKEY'S PAL. June 12, 1912.

178. THE GREAT DISCOVERY. June 14, 1912.

179. FOUR FRIENDS. June 19, 1912.

180. INDIAN SUMMER. June 21, 1912.

181. PLANTING TIME. June 26, 1912.

182. LOVE'S RAILROAD. June 26, 1912.

183. THE CALL OF THE ROSE. June 28, 1912.

184. FATHER AND THE BOYS. July 3, 1912.

185. BETWEEN TWO FIRES. July 5, 1912.

186. WINSOME BUT WISE. July 10, 1912.

187. FRA DIAVOLO. July 12, 1912. 3 reels.

188. HOTEL HONEYMOON. July 12, 1912.

189. SLIPPERY JIM. July 17, 1912.

190. THE FOUR FLUSH ACTOR. July 19, 1912.

191. BROKEN HEARTS. July 24, 1912.

192. THE REQUITAL. July 26, 1912.

193. BOTTLES. July 31, 1912.

194. IMAGINATION. July 31, 1912.

195. BUDDY AND HIS DOG. August 2, 1912.

196. TWO LITTLE RANGERS. August 7, 1912.

197. THE PINK GARTERS. August 9, 1912.

198. THE BLOOD STAIN. August 14, 1912.

199. THE STRIKE. August 16, 1912.

200. THE EQUINE SPY. August 23, 1912.

201. PHANTOM PARADISE. August 28, 1912.

202. PLAYING TRUMPS. August 30, 1912.

203. THE FIGHT IN THE DARK. September 4, 1912.

204. OPEN TO PROPOSALS. September 6, 1912.

205. TREASURES ON THE WING. September 11, 1912.

206. THE SOUL OF THE VIOLIN. Spetember 13, 1912.

207. THE SPRY SPINSTERS. September 18, 1912.

208. THE LIFE OF A ROSE. September 20, 1912.

209. THE LOVE OF THE FLAG. September 25, 1912.

210. THE FUGITIVE. September 27, 1912.

211. SI'S SURPRISE PARTY. October 2, 1912.

212. THE RETREAT FROM EDEN. October 4, 1912.

213. DUBLIN DAN. October 9, 1912.

214. CANNED HARMONY. October 9, 1912.

215. A FOOL AND HIS MONEY. October 11, 1912.

216. THE GOLD BRICK. October 16, 1912.

217. THE MAVERICK. October 18, 1912.

218. THE HIGH COST OF LIVING. October 23, 1912.

219. THE IDOL WORSHIPPER. October 25, 1912.

220. MAKING AN AMERICAN CITIZEN. October 30, 1912.

221. AT THE PHONE. November 1, 1912.

222. THE NEW LOVE AND THE OLD. November 6, 1912.

223. JUST HATS. November 8, 1912.

224. THE PRODIGAL WIFE. November 13, 1912.

225. FLESH AND BLOOD. November 15, 1912.

226. A COMEDY OF ERRORS. November 20, 1912.

227. THE POWER OF MONEY. November 22, 1912.

228. THE PARALYTIC. November 27, 1912.

229. THE JENKINS-PERKINS WAR. November 29, 1912.

230. THE RAFFLE. December 4, 1912.

231. THE FACE AT THE WINDOW. December 6, 1912.

232. THE HATER OF WOMEN. December 11, 1912.

233. THE GIRL IN THE ARMCHAIR. December 13, 1912.

234. HEARTS UNKNOWN. December 18, 1912.

235. FIVE EVENINGS. December 20, 1912.

236. THE FINGER PRINTS. December 25, 1912.

237. THE WOMAN BEHIND THE MAN. December 27, 1912.

238. COUSINS OF SHERLOCK HOLMES. January 1, 1913.

239. CANINE RIVALS. January 3, 1913.

240. A MILLION DOLLARS. January 8, 1913.

241. BEASTS OF THE JUNGLE. January 11, 1913. 3 reels.

242. THE MUTINY OF MR. HENPECK. January 10, 1913.

243. MOTHER AND DAUGHTER. January 15, 1913.

244. THE QUARRELLERS. January 17, 1913.

245. THE COMING OF SUNBEAM. January 22, 1913.

246. THE ROADS THAT LEAD HOME. January 24, 1913.

247. THE WRONG BOX. January 29, 1913.

248. THE SCHEMING WOMAN. January 31, 1913.

249. OVERCOATS. February 4, 1913.

250. THE MONKEY ACCOMPLICE. February 7, 1913.

251. THE EYES OF SATAN. February 12, 1913.

252. THE THIEF. February 14, 1913.

253. BURSTOP HOLMES, DETECTIVE. February 19, 1913.

254. TILL THE DAY BREAKS. February 21, 1913.

255. THE BASHFUL BOY. February 26, 1913.

256. THE VETERAN'S MASCOT. February 28, 1913.

257. DICK WHITTINGTON AND HIS CAT. March 1, 1913.
      3 reels.

258. NAPOLEON. March 5, 1913.

259. THE KISS OF JUDAS. March 7, 1913.

260. WHAT HAPPENED TO OFFICER HENDERSON. March 12, 1913.

261. THE PLANS OF THE HOUSE. March 14, 1913.

262. IN THE WRONG FLAT. March 19, 1913.

263. THE WAY OF THE TRANSGRESSOR. March 21, 1913.

264. BURSTOP HOLMES' MURDER CASE. March 26, 1913.

265. THE CLIMAX. March 28, 1913.

266. THE BACHELOR'S HOUSEKEEPER. April 2, 1913.

267. THE OGRES. April 4, 1913.

268. THE LADY DOCTOR. April 9, 1913.

269. HIS SON-IN-LAW. April 11, 1913.

270. THE MYSTERY OF THE LOST CAT. April 16, 1913.

271. WHERE LOVE DWELLS. April 18, 1913.

272. HIS WIFE'S AFFINITY. April 23, 1913.

273. A SEVERE TEST. April 25, 1913.

274. THE SILVER CROSS. April 30, 1913.

275. A HOUSE DIVIDED. May 2, 1913.

276. THE CASE OF THE MISSING GIRL. May 7, 1913.

277. THE PAST FORGIVEN. May 9, 1913.

278. DAD'S ORDERS. May 14, 1913.

279. THE MAN IN THE SICK ROOM. May 16, 1913.

280. KELLY FROM THE EMERALD ISLE. May 17, 1913. 3 reels.

281. THE AMATEUR HIGHWAYMAN. May 21, 1913.

282. THE MAN WHO FAILED. May 23, 1913.

283. THE HENPECKED BURGLAR. May 28, 1913.

284. THE KING'S MESSENGER. May 30, 1913.

285. THE HOPES OF BELINDA. June 4, 1913.

286. BLOOD AND WATER. June 4, 1913.

287. GREGORY'S SHADOW. June 6, 1913.

288. MATRIMONY'S SPEED LIMIT. June 11, 1913.

289. HER MOTHER'S PICTURE. June 13, 1913.

290. ROMEO IN PAJAMAS. June 18, 1913.

291. STRANGERS FROM NOWHERE. June 20, 1913.

292. THE MERRY WIDOW. June 25, 1913.

293. THE DYNAMITED DOG. June 25, 1913.

294. THE MESSAGE TO HEAVEN. June 27, 1913.

295. AN UNEXPECTED MEETING. July 2, 1913.

296. TRUE HEARTS. July 4, 1913.

297. THE FLEA CIRCUS. July 9, 1913.

298. AS THE BELL RINGS. July 11, 1913.

299. COOKING FOR TROUBLE. July 16, 1913.

300. BRENNAN OF THE MOOR. August. 3 reels.

301. THE INTRUDER. July 18, 1913.

302. THAT DOG. July 23, 1913.

303. AS YE SOW. July 25, 1913.

304. THE COAT THAT CAME BACK. July 30, 1913.

305. WHEN THE TIDE TURNS. August 1, 1913.

306. THE HEAVENLY WIDOW. August 6, 1913.

307. FALSELY ACCUSED. August 8, 1913.

308. FOUR FOOLS AND A MAID. August 13, 1913.

309. A DROP OF BLOOD. August 15, 1913.

310. THE PIT AND THE PENDULUM. August 18, 1913.

311. THE SMUGGLER'S CHILD. August 22, 1913.

312. A TERRIBLE NIGHT. August 27, 1913.

313. A CHILD'S INTUITION. August 29, 1913.

314. MEN AND MUSLIN. September 2, 1913.

315. RETRIBUTION. September 5, 1913.

316. DOOLEY AND HIS DOG. September 10, 1913.

317. GRATITUDE. September 12, 1913.

318. INVISIBLE INK. September 17, 1913.

319. WESTERN LOVE. September 19, 1913.

320. THE QUALITY OF MERCY. September 24, 1913.

321. THE SOUL OF MAN. September 24, 1913.

322. TALE OF A CAT. October 1, 1913.

323. THE LAME MAN. October 3, 1913.

324. BLOOD AND WATER. October 4, 1913. 2 reels.

325. THE LITTLE HUNCHBACK. October 8, 1913.

326. HANDCUFFED FOR LIFE. October 10, 1913.

327. ISH GA BIBBLE. October 15, 1913.

328. FISHERMAN'S LUCK. October 17, 1913.

329. THE ROGUES OF PARIS. October 20, 1913.

330. BEN BOLT. November 22, 1913. 4 reels.

331. SHADOWS OF THE MOULIN ROUGE. December 26, 1913.
     4 reels.

     [THE STAR OF INDIA. Blaché Features, Inc. Released
     November 17, 1913. 4 reels. Although usually
     credited to Alice Guy Blaché, this film appears to
     have been directed by Herbert Blaché.]

     [THE FORTUNE HUNTERS. Blaché Features, Inc.
     Released December 15, 1913. 4 reels. Although
     usually credited to Alice Guy Blaché, this film ap-
     pears to have been directed by Herbert Blaché.]

332. BENEATH THE CZAR. Solax. Released February 1914.
     4 reels. Screenplay: Alice Guy Blaché. With
     Claire Whitney and Fraunie Fraunholz. "Madame
     Blaché has given us a most sensational story in
     films without sacrificing either art or good taste"
     -- The Moving Picture World (February 21, 1914).

333. HOOK AND HAND. Blaché Features, Inc. Released
     February 1914. 4 reels. Screenplay: Francis Wor-
     cester Doughty. Possibly directed by Herbert
     Blaché.

334. THE DREAM WOMAN. Blaché Features, Inc./Box Office
     Attraction Film Rental Company. Released March
     1914. 4 reels. Based on the novel by Wilkie Collins.
     With Claire Whitney and Fraunie Fraunholz. "In
     making the picture, the producer has discarded all
     except what she needed for her peculiar effect. But
     the telling quality of the picture comes most from
     the fact that, by the mysterious alchemy of art she
     changed what material she did use into something
     her own, fresh, new, life-like of today" -- The Mov-
     ing Picture World (March 21, 1914).

335. THE MONSTER AND THE GIRL. Solax. Released March
     25, 1914. 4 reels.

336. THE MILLION DOLLAR ROBBERY. Solax/Blaché Features,
     Inc. Released May 1914. 4 reels. With Claire
     Whitney, Vinnie Burns, Fraunie Fraunholz, and
     James O'Neill. "The staging, the photography and
     the acting, for the most part, are of good quality"
     --The Moving Picture World (June 20, 1914).

337. THE WOMAN OF MYSTERY. Blaché Features, Inc. Re-
     leased May 10, 1914. 4 reels. Screenplay: Alice
     Guy Blaché. With Vinnie Burns, Claire Whitney and
     Fraunie Fraunholz. "A fine picture" -- The Moving
     Picture World (May 30, 1914).

338. THE YELLOW TRAFFIC. Blaché Features, Inc. Re-
     leased June 1914. 4 reels.

339. THE LURE. Blaché Features, Inc./World Film Corpora-
     tion. Released August 24, 1914. 5 reels. Screen-
     play: Alice Guy Blaché, based on the play by George
     Scarborough.

340. THE TIGRESS. Popular Plays and Players/Alco. Re-
     leased December 7, 1914. 4 reels. Screenplay:
     Aaron Hoffman. With Olga Petrova. "The feature
     has a plentitude of thrills, capital acting throughout,
     particularly on the part of Mme. Petrova, who is
     disclosed as a cinema artist of a good deal of power,
     and finally a quantity of highly effective studio
     work" -- Variety (December 25, 1914).

341. THE HEART OF A PAINTED WOMAN. Popular Plays and
     Players/Metro Film Corporation. Released April 19,
     1915. 5 reels. Screenplay: Aaron Hoffman. Photo-
     graphy: Alfred Ortlieb. With Olga Petrova. "A
     good title and a first class dramatic feature" --
     Variety (April 30, 1915).

342. GREATER LOVE HATH NO MAN. Popular Plays and
     Players/Metro Film Corporation. Released July 5,
     1915. 5 reels. Based on the novel by Frank L.
     Packard. Photography: Arthur Ortlieb. With
     Emmett Corrigan, Mary Martin, Thomas Curran,
     Mabel Wright, Crawford Kent, William Morse, and
     Lawrence Grattan.

343. THE VAMPIRE. Popular Plays and Players/Metro Film
     Corporation. Released August 9, 1915. 5 reels.
     Screenplay: Aaron Hoffman, based on the play by
     Edgar Allan Woolf and George Sylvester Viereck.
     With Olga Petrova.

344. MY MADONNA. Popular Plays and Players/Metro Film
     Corporation. Released October 25, 1915. 5 reels.
     Screenplay: Aaron Hoffman, based on the poem in
     "The Spell of the Yukon," by Robert W. Service.
     With Olga Petrova, Guy Coombs, Albert Howson,
     Evelyn Dumo, James O'Neill, Albert Derbill, and
     Yahne Fleury. "At times it is exceptionally artistic,
     revealing ingenuity in the effects attained and a
     skilled use of double exposures"--The Moving Pic-
     ture World (October 23, 1915).

345. WHAT WILL PEOPLE SAY? Popular Plays and Players/
     Metro Film Corporation. Released January 3, 1916.
     5 reels. Screenplay: Aaron Hoffman, based on the
     story by Rupert Hughes. With Olga Petrova, Fraunie
     Fraunholz, Fritz de Lint, Charles Dungan, John
     Dudley, Zadee Burbank, Marilyn Reid, William Morse,
     and Jean Thomas.

     [THE GIRL WITH THE GREEN EYES. Popular Plays and
     Players/Pathé. Released May 15, 1916. 5 reels.
     Although usually credited to Alice Guy Blaché, this
     film appears to have been directed by Herbert
     Blaché].

346. THE OCEAN WAIF. Golden Eagle/International Film Serv-
     ice. Released November 2, 1916. 5 reels. Screen-
     play: Frederick Chapin. Photography: John G.
     Haas. With Carlyle Blackwell, Doris Kenyon, William
     Morse, Fraunie Fraunholz, Lynn Donaldson, August
     Bermeister, and Edgar Norton.

347. THE ADVENTURER. U.S. Amusement Corporation/Art
     Dramas, Inc. Released February 15, 1917. 5 reels.
     Screenplay: Harry Chandlee and Lawrence McCloskey,
     based on the novel by Upton Sinclair. With Marion
     Swayne, Pell Trenton, Charles Halton, Kirke Brown,
     Ethel Stanard, Yolande Doquette, and Martin Hayden.

348. THE EMPRESS. Popular Plays and Players/Pathé. Re-
     leased March 11, 1917. 5 reels. Screenplay: Alice
     Guy Blaché and Holbrook Blinn. Photography: John
     G. Haas. With Doris Kenyon, Holbrook Blinn, William
     Morse, and Lynn Donaldson. "The direction of this
     picture done by Madame Blaché further establishes
     her reputation as an able producer" -- The New York
     Dramatic Mirror (March 3, 1917).

349. A MAN AND THE WOMAN. U.S. Amusement Corporation/
     Art Dramas, Inc. Released March 22, 1917. 5 reels.
     Based on the novel, Nantas, by Emile Zola. Photo-
     graphy: John G. Haas. With Edith Hallor, Leslie
     Austen, and Kirke Brown.

350. HOUSE OF CARDS. U.S. Amusement Corporation/Art
     Dramas, Inc. Released May 31, 1917. 5 reels.
     Screenplay: Alice Guy Blaché. With Catherine
     Calvert, Frank Mills, and James O'Neill.

351. WHEN YOU AND I WERE YOUNG. U.S. Amusement Cor-
     poration/Art Dramas, Inc. Released August 1917.
     5 reels. Based on a story by Frederick Rath.
     Photography: John G. Haas. With Alma Hanlon,
     Harry Benham, and Florence Short.

352. BEHIND THE MASK. U.S. Amusement Corporation/Art
     Dramas, Inc. Released September 3, 1917. 5 reels.
     Screenplay: Charles T. Dazey. Photography: John
     G. Haas. With Catherine Calvert, Richard Tucker,
     Kirke Brown, Charles Dungan, Flora Nason, and
     Charles Holton. "The whole picture is well staged,
     the locations nicely selected. It reflects credit on
     producer Mme. Alice Blaché, who directed" -- Mo-
     tion Picture News (September 29, 1917).

353. THE GREAT ADVENTURE. Pathé. Released March 10,
     1918. 5 reels. Screenplay: Agnes Christine John-
     ston, based on a short story "The Painted Scene"
     by Henry Kitchell Webster. Photography: George
     K. Hollister and John G. Haas. With Bessie Love,
     Chester Barnett, Flora Finch, Donald Hall, Florence
     Short, John W. Dunn, and Walter Craven.

354. TARNISHED REPUTATIONS. Perret/Pathé. Released

March 14, 1920. Producer and Screenplay: Leonce
Perret. Photography: Harry Forbes and Alfred
Ortlieb. With Dolores Cassinelli, Albert Roscoe,
George Deneubourg, and Ned Burton. "The direction of the picture is as faulty as the theme, there
being no care nor discernment used in its development" -- Motion Picture News (March 13, 1920).

Alice Guy Blaché also worked as an assistant director to her
husband on The Divorcee (1919), The Brat (1919), and
Stronger Than Death (1920).